# HOMELAND SECURITY

# HOMELAND SECURITY

## ASSESSING THE FIRST FIVE YEARS

## Michael Chertoff

## Foreword by Lee H. Hamilton

**PENN**

University of Pennsylvania Press

Philadelphia

Published by
University of Pennsylvania Press
Philadelphia, Pennsylvania 19104-4112

Printed in the United States of America on acid-free paper
10  9  8  7  6  5  4  3  2  1

Library of Congress Cataloging-in-Publication Data

Chertoff, Michael, 1953–
Homeland security : assessing the first five years / Michael Chertoff.
        p.    cm.
Includes bibliographical references and index.
ISBN 978-0-8122-4202-7 (alk. paper)
1. United States. Dept. of Homeland Security—Evaluation.
2. National security—United States.  I. Title.
        HV6432.4.C47    2009
    363.34'560973—dc22              2009008428

# Contents

# CONTENTS

# Foreword

## *Lee H. Hamilton*

SINCE the September 11 attacks, the United States government has undergone dramatic reforms. Both during and after my tenure as vice chairman of the 9/11 Commission, I witnessed striking changes, ranging from the restructuring of our intelligence agencies to the creation of the Department of Homeland Security.

These changes, despite some missteps, have generated genuine progress toward better securing the United States. Still, making our homeland more secure is a work in progress. The FBI has made counterterrorism a top priority, fundamentally changing the law enforcement culture and directive of the bureau. An integrated terrorist watch is now complete. Under a new Transportation Security Administration, airline security is tighter. US-VISIT helps ensure that people crossing our borders are who they say they are, though immigration reform remains on the backburner. And Washington, along with state and local governments and the private sector, has invested billions of dollars in protecting our communities and securing critical infrastructure at the federal, state, and local levels.

Notwithstanding these and other efforts, it was the unanimous view of the 9/11 Commission that the United States faced the real prospect of further attacks—a view every expert we consulted in the course of our work shared. Terrorists continue to plot and plan another attack, and in an open and democratic society, defending the country at all times and in all places is practically impossible. Above all, we must not become complacent.

We have yet to endure another terrorist attack on American soil. There are many reasons for that: the weakening of Al Qaeda, financial sanctions, better intelligence, more secure borders, tougher law enforcement, and a host of other steps to better protect the American people. In no small measure, credit belongs to initiatives like the ones I have cited—and to public servants like Michael Chertoff.

As head of the Justice Department's Criminal Division, he led the investigation of the 9/11 attacks. In 2005 he gave up a lifetime federal judicial appointment on the Third Circuit to become the nation's second secretary of homeland security. There is always debate in Washington about what is the second toughest job in town. My candidate would be secretary of homeland security.

As a member of the Homeland Security Advisory Council, I have come to know Michael Chertoff as an able and intelligent man of integrity and vision. His energy, professionalism, and sustained commitment helped him handle with great aplomb the daunting task at hand: making the component agencies of DHS, some with proud and illustrious histories, work together under a common mission. Since the baton recently has been passed to a new administration and secretary, it is now especially appropriate to commend his contributions to the nation's safety and security.

This book is itself a valuable addition to our understanding of homeland security and a much needed explanation of some of America's post-9/11 policies. As such, it is educational. Americans need to know more about homeland security, and throughout this book, its author proves an able teacher.

America's approach to counterterrorism might be summed up as follows. First, we assess the threats terrorists pose. Armed with that assessment, we take steps to prevent and protect against future attacks. Recognizing that we cannot be everywhere at once, we prioritize in hopes of minimizing the risk of attack, rather than engage in futile and counterproductive attempts to eliminate every threat imaginable. Well aware that despite our best efforts another attack remains possible, we plan and prepare for a response that will minimize its costs. And understanding the global nature of terrorism, we know we cannot go at it alone, so we cultivate relations with our friends and allies overseas. Each of these steps is difficult. We have not executed them perfectly, but progress has been made in all of them. That is our nation's strategy, and it is one that this book lays out with clarity and precision.

One of the first axioms of any conflict is to know one's enemy. In our battle against terrorism, we must not only know the identity of our foes, but understand the ideology that fuels their desire to harm us—and counter it.

Weakening terrorists and their sponsors and eliminating safe havens are necessary but not sufficient. We must engage in the battle of ideas, speaking and listening to the world's Muslims in the struggle to win hearts and minds. We must be sensitive to their hopes, dreams, and concerns. And we must explain our values and our policies. We must put forward an agenda of opportunity, one that supports pragmatic political reform, as well as education, the rule of law, civil society, and economic empowerment.

With all of his skills in orchestrating the budgetary and organizational challenges of homeland security, Michael Chertoff did not neglect these broader and fundamental aspects of the effort to secure America. This book underscores how crucial they are and will continue to be. Rejecting the notion that military might alone can win the day, he displays a genuine understanding of how our security depends on successfully integrating and utilizing all the tools of American power in defense of our national interests.

This volume has many strong qualities, but I will highlight a few. First, as exemplified by his balanced discussion of missteps prior to 9/11, this book transcends partisanship and instead identifies the structural obstacles that confront policy-makers in any administration.

Second, the author is not self-congratulatory. This book, although reflective and retrospective at points, is ultimately forward-looking. It warns of looming perils, the need to confront threats, close vulnerabilities, and resist a spirit of national complacency, a perennial obstacle to common-sense policies that can help make us safe.

And yet, while this book warns against the risks of complacency, it exhibits an admirable balance by rejecting the opposite extreme: total risk elimination. Not only is that aim unachievable, but an across-the-board pursuit of it would court disaster. It could shutter our commerce, threaten our liberties and way of life, and hand the terrorists a critical victory. The way to combat complacency is to work tirelessly against opposition to sound policies rooted in proven risk management principles. Such policies aim to prevent attacks and also to plan and prepare for an effective response should attacks occur.

By discussing these matters candidly and straightforwardly, and by puncturing associated myths, legends, and wrongheaded notions about homeland security, Michael Chertoff does the reader, and the nation, a service. One of the greatest myths is the idea that in combating terrorism, America is or should be a Lone Ranger nation. In response to this assertion, this book cites impressive examples of how we and our allies are not only working closely together, but have enacted remarkably similar security policies, from biometrics to secure identification.

Clearly, this book is a notable and important addition to our ongoing national discourse and understanding about homeland security from one of the country's most informed and distinguished public servants. It is also a welcome reminder of his accomplishments.

# Introduction

I N March 2008, the United States commemorated the fifth anniversary of the creation of the Department of Homeland Security. The occasion was marked by a historic event in the nation's capital, at which I hosted President George W. Bush and my predecessor, Tom Ridge, along with thousands of dedicated men and women of the department.

This volume highlights the achievements of the Department of Homeland Security since its founding, along with its continued challenges in relation to its mission. That mission is to pursue a unified, risk-managed strategy of preventing or reducing America's vulnerability to terrorism and natural disasters, a strategy designed to guard the nation and its infrastructure from dangerous people and material, while mitigating the consequences of disasters by strengthening the nation's emergency preparedness and response systems.

Certainly the first step in preventing or mitigating the risk of disaster is to know and understand the dangers we face. Accordingly, the book's initial section catalogues the known threats to the homeland. It spells out both natural and man-made threats, from tornados to terrorism.

Concerning the terrorist threat, the September 11 attacks compelled us to recognize the growing power of an extremist global movement, one that had birthed a series of networked organizations dedicated to the destruction of America, its institutions, and its way of life. Who were these dangerous individuals and groups? What were their fundamental objectives and goals? What motivated them to destroy the lives of nearly 3,000 innocent civilians on that fateful day? What level of threat will they likely pose to our homeland for the foreseeable future?[1]

In Chapter 1, "Assessing the Dangers," I discuss these sworn enemies of our nation and of its friends and allies. While identifying Al Qaeda as the principal threat, I also depict organizations like Hezbollah as having the motivation and capabilities to pose a serious risk to our security over the next generation. I also discuss the emerging threat posed by transnational gangs like MS-13. These increasingly sophisticated criminal organizations engage in drug and human trafficking, kidnapping, and murder-for-hire. They pose an immediate danger to the stability of governments in our hemisphere and have the potential to evolve into ideological organizations with political objectives that are similar to those of international terrorist groups.

In Chapter 2, "The Ideological Roots of Terror," I identify and explore the historical roots of radical Islamism, the ideology that drives our foes. Pointing to the surprisingly Western, totalitarian roots of this extremism, I describe how it threatens Western democracy and traditional Islam alike. Clearly, we are opposed not merely by a physical enemy, but by this virulent ideology. I portray the fight against global terrorism as a contest between the ideals of freedom and those of tyranny. Like the Cold War, this struggle will likely last for decades. It is a global battle for hearts and minds as well as territory, and its outcome will depend on our ability to resist complacency and retain our resolve and belief in the rightness of our cause.

A final point must be made about the threats America faces to its safety. Homeland security deals not only with terrorism and related dangers, but also with natural threats like hurricanes and floods, wildfires and tornados. Unlike man-made threats, these obviously cannot be prevented from occurring. We can and should, however, continue to take action to minimize their likely impact. This will be explored in later chapters. Once we have identified and explored the nature of these threats to our safety and security, we can devise and adopt an aggressive, effective approach to prevention. That approach is set forth in the second section of this book, Prevention.

In our efforts to prevent terrorist attacks and other disasters from occurring, our first and foremost priority is to keep dangerous individuals from entering our country or to remove those who are already here. Part of that strategy involves what we do at our nation's borders. An essential part of homeland security must involve border security, which includes reducing the number of individuals who enter illegally. And it also involves interior enforcement—dealing with people who are already here illegally. Porous borders are an engraved invitation to terrorists, gang members, criminal fugitives, and drug and human traffickers to come here and do harm. Yet most individuals who have crossed our borders came for economic reasons and pose no physical danger to the country.

In Chapter 3, "Securing the Border—and Reforming Immigration," I advocate a two-pronged approach to the problem. First, we must make our borders more secure. This we are doing by building pedestrian and vehicular fencing and deploying more manpower and technology, particularly at our southern border. And second, Congress needs to pass comprehensive immigration reform, in part to free our border patrol and immigration enforcement officers to spend more time pursuing truly dangerous people.

While protecting the nation's borders is paramount, our borders are not our sole line of defense. Our aim is to deal with the threat posed by dangerous people before as well as after they arrive. This requires the deployment of a number of vital tools or options. Chapter 4, "Using Every Tool," lays out an array of options available to the U.S. government to prevent acts of terrorism from being visited on America. They range from the military option, deployed against the Taliban in Afghanistan and Al Qaeda in Iraq, to information and intelligence gathering and sharing, to law enforcement tools used against terrorists whom we have prosecuted in our civilian criminal courts. But the most promising preventive tool of all is highlighted in Chapter 5, "Why Soft Power Works."

What is soft power? It refers to the various humanitarian, political, and economic activities we are engaged in throughout the world, actions that may not only reduce terrorist recruitment but wean hearts and minds away from radical ideologies and to a more hopeful, democratic future. Why is soft power the best preventive tool? The reason is simple. The best way to prevent terrorism is to attract people to alternatives to terrorism and to its animating ideology.

For many people, any discussion of preventive measures against terrorism begs the obvious question: Why was the United States unable to prevent the 9/11 attacks? In Chapter 6, "Why Washington Won't Work," I identify what I call structural obstacles as part of the answer. Basically, every official in government is confronted by a set of powerful impediments to advancing the national interest. In this chapter, I explore some of these obstacles, how they helped derail pre-9/11 efforts to deal with looming dangers, and how we are working hard to counter these obstacles in the future.

While preventing people from launching attacks has been an integral part of our strategy for securing the homeland, it is not the only part. The third section in this volume, Protection: Reducing Vulnerabilities, focuses on the need to identify its vulnerabilities to disasters, natural as well as man-made, and then reduce them.

In Chapter 7, "Protecting and Preserving Infrastructure," I highlight the need to protect key structures, from chemical facilities to other essential national assets. Since most of the country's critical physical infrastructure is owned and operated by private individuals and businesses, top-down government micromanagement is not the solution. The answer is for government to issue safety and security goals and timetables and then let these individuals and businesses determine how to meet them. This has been our fundamental strategy in dealing with every sector of our economy, most notably the chemical industry. The chapter also tackles the nationwide problem of infrastructure maintenance. What good is it to protect critical infrastructure from a terrorist attack, only to see it crumble due to lack of preventive maintenance? Most of the damage to New Orleans in 2005 from Hurricane Katrina was caused by the collapse of levees that had been inadequately maintained.

In Chapter 8, "Cybersecurity," I lay out the special problems and risks confronting our cyber infrastructure. At stake are not only commercial and governmental operations, but also such crucial concerns as the uninterrupted functioning of the nation's power grid.

In Chapter 9, "Responding to IEDs at Home," I deal with the domestic threat posed by improvised explosive devices (IEDs). These range from conventional explosives to so-called dirty bombs containing radioactive material capable of contaminating the areas in which they are detonated. Unlike a nuclear weapon, an IED is relatively simple to assemble and its materials easy to obtain, which is partly why it has long been the terrorist weapon of choice throughout the world.

In Chapter 10, "Managing Identity," I discuss another vulnerability that terrorists and others who seek our harm are attempting to exploit, namely identity. The problem of identity theft and fraud has been increasing dramatically over time, and I suggest some practical answers that will likely be applied as technology advances.

Despite our diligent efforts to guard the nation from disasters, the stark reality is that total avoidance of them is ultimately impossible. In fact, a strategy that is designed for this purpose will not only fail, but will be self-defeating. For example, if we wished to eliminate the risk of airliners being blown up, we could shut down all the airports. But that would destroy the airline industry and much of our commerce, effectively handing the terrorists the victory they seek.

It is neither possible nor desirable to pursue a risk elimination strategy. Instead, we must do two things. First, we must adopt a strategy that seeks to manage rather than eliminate risks. Second, we must engage in preparedness planning so that when disasters do happen, we can respond in a manner that minimizes the consequences, saving as many lives as possible.

The fourth section, Preparation and Response, deals both with risk management and with the need to prepare and plan for the possibility of catastrophic events and respond when they occur. In Chapter 11, "Managing Risk," I make the case for a more sensible and strategic approach to risk, not just for the United States but for the world. I cite three key areas in which government must step in and help people and businesses handle risk more effectively. However, I caution against a mindset of overregulation driven by the fruitless quest for risk elimination.

The need for comprehensive emergency planning can be readily seen when we examine the risks of unleashing weapons of mass destruction against our country. In terms of consequence, there is no greater threat than that of a nuclear device being detonated in one of our major cities. A more likely event, however, and one that deserves greater consideration than it gets, is a biological incident. In Chapter 12, "Biological Threats and Bioterrorism," I survey the challenges and possible consequences of unleashing a biological agent in the United States. Our society has prepared in various ways for such an event, but it clearly must do more, and the time to do more is today.

No discussion of national preparedness and response is complete without examining the role played by the Federal Emergency Management Agency (FEMA). In Chapter 13, "The Question of FEMA and Homeland Security," I focus on FEMA's crucial role in that arena. Unfortunately, there are some who argue for removing FEMA from DHS. I make the case that FEMA must stay. FEMA remains an integral part of the overall mission of DHS and can pursue its own mission far better under the DHS umbrella than alone.

The final section of this volume, International Dimensions, covers our recognition of the international dimensions of the risks we face. In the twenty-first-century global environment, people, goods, money, and ideas crisscross the world in a matter of seconds and hours, rather than days and weeks. Unfortunately, so can terrorists. We need look no further than to 9/11, where the plot was hatched in Central Asia, using recruits from Saudi Arabia who trained in Afghanistan and planned in Europe before launching their attack in America.

Clearly, the threat we face from our foes remains a global one, requiring strong partnerships with friends and allies overseas. Most nations, including those of Europe, certainly grasp the danger terrorism poses to them and to our entire system of security, safety and prosperity. They recall the post-9/11 bombings in Madrid and in the United Kingdom, and the thwarted plot revealed in London in the summer of 2006 against transatlantic airliners. Yet a myth has developed that America is diverging from the rest of the world in the fight against terrorism. As one who has worked closely and extensively as DHS secretary with my security counterparts abroad, I can attest to the contrary.

In Chapter 14, "Cooperation and Consensus Abroad," I cite broad areas of agreement with our overseas democratic partners on the threat we face and how we must counter it. Nation after nation is implementing the same strategies and programs in the effort to prevent terrorists from striking their populations. Strategically, they are increasingly agreeing to extend their security perimeters abroad, coordinate their efforts, and strive to manage their security risks rather than ignoring or trying to eliminate them. And in three key areas—passenger data collection, biometrics, and secure traveler identification—our partners abroad have been implementing the same kinds of programs as our own.

In working with our partners on security matters, I have had ample occasion to deal with international law. I have concluded that there is a fundamental problem with much of its current architecture. In Chapter 15, "The Responsibility to Contain," I make the case for international legal reform. Specifically, nations need both freedom and accountability in response to terrorism. This does not contradict their need to partner with each other against our common foe. Rather, it acknowledges that every nation is confronted by a developing framework of international law that can often be a hindrance rather than a help to our collective security needs.

# THREATS

# Assessing the Dangers

Like other nations, the United States has always faced threats to its safety and security. In recent years, however, our media have breathlessly conveyed the impression that threats of nearly every kind are materializing with far greater frequency than in the past. This is partly an illusion triggered by a human tendency to magnify today's problems compared with those of yesterday. What is hardly illusory is the outworking of a number of distinctly modern developments that give rise to emerging vulnerabilities.

When it comes to natural threats, for example, we have built communities in areas susceptible to wildfires, earthquakes, and floods, putting record numbers of people at risk. Moreover, the globalization of modern travel has produced unprecedented geographical mobility, raising the specter of a worldwide spread of infectious diseases. With respect to man-made threats, the mobility that can deliver diseases to our doorstep can bring terrorism there as well. In addition, modern science and technology amplify the capabilities of terrorists so that they may someday have the potential to destroy countless lives by detonating a single weapon in a well-populated area.

What can we do about these emerging threats to the homeland? In dealing with natural threats, we can stop some diseases in their tracks through inoculation, but obviously, we cannot prevent earthquakes or hurricanes. What we can do is take steps to reduce our vulnerability and improve our capacity to respond to them. And in the case of man-made dangers, there is much that we can do to prevent disasters from occurring. But it is imperative that we first identify and face squarely the nature and extent of those perils.

## Threats Man-Made

For much of the last century, the United States and the Soviet Union existed under the threat of nuclear annihilation. As the famous *Bulletin of the Atomic Scientists* doomsday clock illustrated, we grew sometimes closer to and sometimes more distant from the midnight of an apocalypse. Yet this system was remarkably and fundamentally stable. It rested on the understanding that our Soviet adversaries had as much to lose from a nuclear exchange as we did. They had no desire to become martyrs. This system was sufficiently sturdy that it changed only when the internal structure of the Soviet system crumbled.

In the new century, we face challenges that are obviously different in a number of ways. Terrorist groups do not wield destructive power remotely on the scale of a nuclear state. But networked terrorists also act without the restraints of deterrence. Their supporters and assets are dispersed and low profile. Their willingness to be martyred is significant. And modern technology has given even small groups a destructive potential that continues to increase.

Nevertheless, there is a commonality between the current threat of terrorism and the historical challenge posed by the Soviet Union and other communist powers. It is the need to confront a unified, underlying ideology and worldview. In confronting the Soviets, we faced the ideology of Marxism, however hollow it eventually appeared. In our struggle with international terrorism, our main adversary is a cult of violent Islamist extremism, which seeks to hijack for its own ends the religion of hundreds of millions of peaceful Muslims. In the case of Marxism, what began as a movement distributed in pockets around the globe led to an ideology that took control of nations. In like manner, violent Islamist extremists seek host states in which they can train, flourish, and create platforms from which to attack other countries. Their aim is to follow the example of Marxism by gaining control of states or nations. This similarity is no accident. An Al Qaeda training document discovered in Afghanistan in 2002 specifically referred to Mao Zedong's three stages of insurgency: (1) recruitment and indoctrination; (2) sustained terrorist warfare; and (3) the ultimate seizure of territory and the levers of state power. Of course, Al Qaeda came closest to achieving the third and final stage of power during its pre-9/11 alliance with the Taliban in Afghanistan.

More recently, leaders of this extremist ideology have reiterated this goal. Ayman al-Zawahiri, Osama bin Laden's deputy, proclaimed in July 2006 on an extremist web site that "the whole world is an open field for us." And the uncompromising view of these radicals is made clear by a line in Al Qaeda's charter that reads as follows: "We will not meet the enemy halfway and there will be no room to dialogue with them." In order to grasp fully the implications of such rhetoric, we need only recall the conditions in Afghanistan under the Taliban. They harbored Al Qaeda, inflicted horrific punishment on dissenters, and drove women from public life, making them the virtual property of husbands and fathers and denying them an education along with other rights recognized by the modern world. It was only through the overthrow of that regime that these rights were restored.

But the destruction of Al Qaeda's headquarters in Afghanistan—while a major positive step—did not obliterate this terrorist organization or the virulent ideology it represents. Following this substantial setback, Al Qaeda and its key members retreated to other parts of the world. They removed to the frontier areas of Pakistan, where over time they have obtained breathing space to train, plan, experiment, and maintain a pipeline of operatives. They extended into the Maghreb in North Africa, and carried out attacks against UN facilities, courts, and schoolchildren. They have returned to parts of Somalia, whose weakened government produced a climate conducive to lawlessness, including piracy on the high seas. In Somalia, Al Qaeda and its cohorts hope to control territory and increase their capability of launching further attacks.

When we outline the continued threats we face from terrorism, we must begin with an extremist ideology and with Al Qaeda, its most potent representative. Vice-Admiral J. Michael McConnell, U.S. director of intelligence in the second Bush administration, noted, "Al Qaeda remains the pre-eminent threat against the United States, both here at home and abroad."[1] Indeed, Al Qaeda and its affiliates form a truly global terrorist network, with a presence on multiple continents. While Al Qaeda remains a significant threat to the U.S. homeland, it continues to target societies across the Muslim world that reject its message and its methodology. It has launched numerous attacks against Muslims with ferocity and contempt for human life and dignity.

Al Qaeda and similar groups have killed thousands of people, mostly Muslims, over the past several years. Among their targets have been political candidates and government leaders. In December 2007, the assassination of Benazir Bhutto by Al Qaeda-allied militants brutally ended her quest to become Pakistan's elected leader again. In February 2008, in Rawalpindi, near Pakistan's capital, a suicide bombing killed that country's surgeon general. Also in February, an Al Qaeda plot was uncovered to assassinate the president of the Philippines.

But these extremists have seen fit to murder ordinary citizens as well. In November 2005, in Amman, Jordan, a bride and groom and the fathers of the two newlyweds were among the dozens of Muslims slaughtered in the middle of a wedding celebration by a triple suicide bombing. In April 2008, in a town north of Baghdad, at least forty-five people were killed during a funeral for two Sunni tribesmen.

Every report of wanton killings by Al Qaeda and its affiliates serves as a grim reminder of the lethal threat they pose. But here is the vulnerability that Al Qaeda has now created for itself: this unending slaughter of innocent Muslims sows the potential seeds for Al Qaeda's failure. Simply stated, these acts of extremism are alienating the very pool of people terrorists wish to convert to their creed. Tellingly, the two Sunni tribesmen mentioned above were part of an Awakening Council that was battling Al Qaeda and its minions in Iraq. Within the Sunni sections of Iraq, there has been a rising tide of revulsion against the mounting atrocities of Al Qaeda and other foreign fighters. Sunni leaders have taken up arms to free themselves from these terrorists. Coupled with the American military surge, the result has been a dramatic setback for Al Qaeda in Iraq.

This undeniable backlash against the extremists is not limited to Iraq. Clerics and other Muslim leaders around the world have begun a dialogue in which the apologetic for violence is emphatically rejected. Salman al Oudah, a well-known Saudi cleric, sent an open letter to bin Laden in 2007 criticizing Al Qaeda's attacks against innocent civilians. In his letter, Oudah asked, "How many innocents among children, elderly, the weak, and women have been killed and made homeless in the name of Al Qaeda?"[2] As a result, potential recruits to violent Islamic extremism are hearing an alternative view with growing clarity. They are beginning to learn from respected clerics that those who would recruit them to a creed that glorifies death and destruction are offering a false path.

Individual Muslims are now questioning Al Qaeda's indiscriminate violence. In a web-based question-and-answer session, al-Zawahiri was forced to strike a defensive tone in the face of sharp questioning of bombings that killed innocent Muslims, including schoolchildren.[3] One questioner asked, "Do you consider the killing of women and children to be jihad?" In response to such questions, al-Zawahiri became defensive, alternately denying the charges, claiming that some of the innocents had been used as shields, and awkwardly insisting that Al Qaeda is entitled to destroy people who get in the way of their operations. Coupled with other Al Qaeda statements designed to discredit Muslim religious leaders who are opposing them, it appears that Al Qaeda's leaders are becoming worried about the growing, active opposition from within the Muslim community.

These are significant developments in the battle against extremism and terrorism. Every effort we make to counter the terrorist threat will fail if terrorist groups are able to recruit operatives faster than we can capture or kill them. Clearly, in the long run, the war against terrorism will be largely won or lost in the recruitment arena. The threat of violent Islamist extremism will not soon pass. Al Qaeda will continue pursuing platforms, recruitment and training opportunities, and laboratories in which to experiment with weapons. Therefore we dare not abandon our vigilance. In the short run, capturing and killing Al Qaeda leaders and operatives; frustrating the flow of their communications, money, and travel; and disrupting their plots are crucial tasks. But the strategic battle will be for the allegiance of a critical mass of Muslims. In that effort, the fulcrum must be a growing counterforce to extremism. It cannot emerge from governments or from their leaders in the West. It must come from within the Muslim community, finding its voice and rejecting the attempts to hijack Islam.

Although Al Qaeda and its network are our most serious immediate threat, they may not be our most serious long-term threat. There are other terrorist organizations, also driven by radical beliefs and practices, that pose a strategic risk to our nation and its allies. Among them is Hezbollah, a word that literally means the "party of God." Hezbollah has a history that reaches back to the early 1980s, with its creation as a pro-Iranian Shi`a militia. Long before Al Qaeda was formed, Hezbollah had helped pioneer suicide bombing, including the 1983 bombing of U.S. Marine peacekeepers in Lebanon and the 1996 bombing of the Khobar Towers in Saudi Arabia.

Former deputy secretary of state Richard Armitage once called Hezbollah "the A-team of terrorists," and for good reason.[4] Having operated for more than a quarter-century, it has developed capabilities about which Al Qaeda can only dream, including large quantities of missiles and highly sophisticated explosives, uniformly well-trained operatives, an exceptionally well-disciplined military force of nearly 30,000 fighters, and extraordinary political influence. Hezbollah shows what an ideologically driven terrorist organization can become when it evolves into an army and a political party and gains a deeply embedded degree of control within a state, as Hezbollah has done in Lebanon's democratic infrastructure. This is, in many ways, a terrorist group that has "graduated" from Mao's second stage of insurgency to the third stage, where it is steps away from ruling part or all of a functioning nation-state. Indeed, looking ahead, there is a real danger that Hezbollah could paralyze or even dismember Lebanon.

The good news is that Hezbollah's alliance with hostile foreign powers like Iran and Syria has cost it the support of hundreds of thousands of Lebanese citizens who especially resent Syria's history of encroachments on Lebanon's sovereignty. While Hezbollah may not have carried out attacks in the United States itself, it has developed a presence in the Western Hemisphere, specifically in South America. In 1992, it bombed the Israeli embassy in Buenos Aires, killing twenty-nine people. Two years later, it murdered eighty-five people by bombing a Jewish community center in that city. These acts disturbingly underscore Hezbollah's reach into the hemisphere, notably in the tri-border areas at the margins of Brazil, Argentina, and Paraguay. Hezbollah's patron, Iran, is also forging warmer relations with Venezuela. These developments, only a relatively short distance from U.S. borders, highlight the fact that Hezbollah is not just a Middle Eastern concern.

In our immediate backyard other terrorist groups with different ideologies also pose a threat. Among the oldest is the Revolutionary Armed Forces of Colombia, or FARC (Fuerzas Armadas Revolucionarias de Colombia). Starting in the 1960s as a Marxist guerrilla group that took up arms against the government, it eventually became a criminal enterprise as well. Today, it engages in a host of activities, from narcotics trafficking and extortion to kidnapping and hostage taking for ransom and political leverage, in order to fuel its ideological efforts and its protracted war against Colombia's duly elected government. Organized along military lines, FARC replicates in the areas it controls the influence that Hezbollah has in parts of Lebanon or that Al Qaeda once had in Afghanistan. Like Al Qaeda and Hezbollah, it is listed by the State Department as a foreign terrorist organization. And FARC demonstrates what happens when terrorism and organized crime converge, each enabling the other.

FARC has clear ties to President Hugo Chávez's Venezuelan government and has been hosted by Chávez in that country. When Colombian forces killed a key FARC leader in early 2008, they found computer files that suggested even closer ties with Venezuela than previously known. This connection between a terrorist group and a nation-state notably parallels the relationship between Hezbollah and Iran. And as with Al Qaeda and Hezbollah, FARC has generated significant opposition among the people whose allegiance it seeks. Millions of Colombians rallied against it in early 2008, demanding that it release the hundreds of hostages it has been holding for years.

Finally, while Al Qaeda, Hezbollah, and FARC represent threats from ideologically motivated organizations, U.S. security will be increasingly threatened as well by sophisticated transnational groups that operate purely as criminal enterprises. The same forces of globalization that have helped spread dangerous ideologies have empowered criminal organizations to become far more adept at trafficking in narcotics and human beings, and also in other kinds of activities that threaten the stability of societies and their governments.

Perhaps the most lethal of such groups is Mara Salvatrucha, MS-13, formed in the early 1980s by immigrants in Los Angeles, some of whom were former guerrilla fighters in El Salvador. It began as a street gang, selling illegal narcotics, committing violent crimes, and fighting turf wars with other criminal entities. In January 2008, an FBI threat assessment noted that MS-13 is in at least forty-two of our fifty states, with 6,000 to 10,000 members nationwide. Over time, MS-13 has spread not only across our cities but back into Central America, engaging in human trafficking, assassinations for hire, assaults on law enforcement officials, and other violent activities that threaten the stability of countries in that region.

In 1997, in Honduras, MS-13 kidnapped and murdered the son of President Ricardo Maduro. In 2002, in the Honduran city of Tegucigalpa, MS-13 members boarded a bus, executed twenty-eight people (including seven small children), and left a handwritten message taunting the government. Two years later, the president of Guatemala, Oscar Berger, received a message tied to the body of a dismembered man, warning of more killings to come.

MS-13 is not now an ideological group, but it continues to bring death and disorder to our neighbors to the south. That will be even more disturbing should a day come when this criminal network gains the power to dominate a small state in our own hemisphere.

## The Generational Challenge

From Al Qaeda to MS-13, over the next decade we will face a full spectrum of man-made threats that call for an array of preventive measures. These threats will derive from organizations that are networked, widely distributed, difficult to deter, and aided in their ability to commit acts of violence by globalization and technological advances in travel, communications, and weaponry.

How will we prevent such threats from being carried out against our country? In brief, we need to keep pursuing a broad-gauged strategy. First, we need to keep using our military and intelligence assets abroad to stop dangerous people from reaching us at home. Second, we need to secure those hinges of the global architecture that are being exploited by global terrorism and crime, and where these illegal global networks are also at their most vulnerable. This means intercepting the illegal networks' communications, stopping their flow of finance, and interfering with their ability to travel.

Third, wherever we face ideological threats, we must contend with them. We must give voice to those around the world who oppose them. From Iraq to Lebanon to the Western Hemisphere, wherever people stand for freedom against tyranny and terror, we must stand with them. And we must urge communities of moderation to have the courage of their convictions and take a similar stand. To do anything less is to cede the battlefield of ideas to extremists, enabling them to recruit the next generation of terrorists without a fight. Fourth, we need to encourage the free flow of people and ideas to and from our nation. That means outreach to encourage travel to the United States

Fifth, we must continue to send people and resources abroad to help meet humanitarian needs. When we help African nations fight malaria or HIV/AIDS, we are not only combating misery with compassion, but demonstrating our values through positive action. Hezbollah gained significant traction by providing social services to local communities. When we have provided aid overseas, as in post-tsunami Asia, we have seen our image strengthened. Engagement with health, education, and social welfare around the globe can be an important tool in strengthening global security.

Finally, enhancing our trade and security support for our international partners is critical in fostering the strength they need to resist dangerous global ideologies and criminal networks. Whether through free-trade agreements like the one with Colombia or capacity-building plans like the Merida Initiative aimed at reinforcing Mexico's campaign against narcotraffickers, we must seize every opportunity to inoculate our neighbors against international terrorists and crime organizations.

Unquestionably, the threats we face constitute a generational challenge to our nation—a challenge we can surely meet and overcome through patient and sustained resolve, a common-sense strategy, and a comprehensive set of intelligent policies and tools.

# The Ideological Roots
of Terror

S INCE the September 11 attacks, the United States has continued to confront the threat posed by its terrorist foes. In the summer of 2006, for example, a major plot to hijack transatlantic airliners was disrupted in London. It served as a stark reminder of how our enemies continue to target this nation and its allies.

In response to this threat, the United States and its friends must maintain their vigilance against terrorism. But they must also combat the ideas that drive the terrorists. As Jonathan Evans, director general of the British Security Service, has said, "Although the most visible manifestations of this problem are the attacks and attempted attacks we have suffered in recent years, the root of the problem is ideological."[1] Al Qaeda and like-minded organizations are inspired by a malignant ideology, one that is characterized by contempt for human dignity and freedom and a depraved disregard for human life.

The terrorists claim that they are practicing Islam, but in the words of Bernard Lewis, one of the foremost Western scholars of Islam, "At no point do the basic texts of Islam enjoin terrorism and murder. At no point do they even consider the random slaughter of uninvolved bystanders."[2] Indeed, an increasing number of Muslim scholars and clerics have voiced the same objection to conflating Islam with extremists who claim to act in its name.

What, then, is the ideology of the terrorists who commit acts of mass murder against non-Muslims and Muslims alike? What is it that distinguishes the violent extremism of bin Laden and his fellow travelers not only from modern, Western democracy, but from normative, historical Islam? In large measure, this ideology is influenced by twentieth-century Western totalitarianism.

## Modern Parallels: Radical Islam and Western Totalitarianism

There are at least four indicators that point to a connection between today's extremists and their early and mid-twentieth-century intellectual cousins who advanced totalitarian ideologies such as communism and fascism.

The first of these is the language used by today's virulent extremist leaders. To a remarkable degree, it mimics the radical rhetoric of the last century. Words like "vanguard" and "revolution" are used for self-definition, whereas "imperialist," "capitalist," "colonialist," "reactionary," and "establishment" are hurled at enemies, from the United States to mainstream Muslim leaders. To cite a relatively recent example, in September 2007 an extremist website posted links to a video message from bin Laden to the people of the United States. In that message, Al Qaeda's leader called U.S. officials "war criminals" and labeled the U.S. media a "tool of the colonialist empires." He also railed against "the shackles . . . of the capitalist system" and implied that "big corporations" agitate for war, despoil the environment, and had President John F. Kennedy killed.[3]

This rhetoric is, of course, familiar as that of ideological extremists of the last century. And this use of the jargon of Western radicalism is not restricted to Al Qaeda or to other Sunni extremist groups. The Shi`a-dominated movement led by the late Ayatollah Ruhollah Khomeini, which brought down the Shah in Iran thirty years ago, remains a case in point. To this day, Iran's ruling movement calls its own efforts "the revolution" and, through bestowing names like the "Revolutionary Guards" on its institutions, it advertises itself as a radicalizing force.

This is not to deny that these groups superficially deploy the rhetoric of conventional Islam as well. They certainly do, but they utilize a decidedly ideological and political framework. A noteworthy example is their distortion of the word "jihad." As interpreted by traditional Muslim scholars and clerics, jihad speaks of the spiritual struggle against sin. While that can include literally fighting an enemy, even when it does, it comes with rules that bar indiscriminate killing. Much of the time, however, the word refers to the believer's internal striving for self-improvement. But in the lexicon of Islamist extremists, it has come to connote acts of prodigious violence against governments that are deemed non-Muslim or insufficiently Islamic. Worse, it has come to include the launching of deliberate attacks against innocent civilians—in other words, terrorism. And it includes the most barbaric method of terrorism: suicide bombing.

Clearly, then, the rhetoric of Islamist extremists, even when it uses Muslim terminology, evokes a set of norms and tactics that depart from a traditional understanding of Islam in crucial ways. It points to a worldview that is similar to twentieth-century communism and fascism. These extremists mistreat Islam as a political ideology. In so doing, they echo the ideas of other ideologues who sought a radical reordering of society and the world, achieved through the violent overthrow of the existing order by perpetrating mass violence against civilians as well as traditional combatants.

Indiscriminate violence is a second way that today's Islamist radicalism carries on the legacy of revolutionary Marxism and fascism. Borrowing from those extremist ideologies, it rejects *on principle* the distinction between combatants and noncombatants in the conduct of war. In bin Laden's own words, spoken to a U.S. reporter in 1998, "we do not have to differentiate between military or civilian. As far as we are concerned, they are all targets."[4]

From the perspective of totalitarian ideologues, societies that reject the call for total revolutionary transformation are fair game. Their governments are considered thoroughly corrupt and evil, as are their ordinary citizens. Wherever the status quo persists, totalitarian extremists deem war a revolutionary necessity, and war on civilians morally justifiable. From fascists in Europe to Maoists in Cambodia, the twentieth century is filled with stark examples. Thus, a morally fanatical premise—that if "the system" is wicked, so is every participant—leads to a morally bankrupt outcome like the 9/11 atrocities. We need only recall the chilling words of Ward Churchill, the radical professor formerly at the University of Colorado, who likened the World Trade Center's doomed office workers to "little Eichmanns."[5]

Third, besides adopting Western radicalism's distinctive patterns of thought and speech and its rationale for unrestrained violence, Islamist extremism also shares its macabre celebration of death. Comparing his own ideology with that of the United States not long after the 9/11 attacks, bin Laden said, "We love death. The U.S. loves life. That is the difference between us two."[6]

As a number of observers have noted, the celebration of death was a particularly striking feature of early Western totalitarian movements. A famous instance occurred in 1936, at the University of Salamanca in Spain, when José Millán-Astray, a pro-Nazi general, shouted at an opponent, "Viva la Muerte!," "Long Live Death."[7] One of the mottos of Benito Mussolini's National Fascist Party was "Viva la Morte," which means the same thing in Italian.

Totalitarianism has drawn deeply from the Jacobin notion that mass bloodletting, when unleashed by a revolutionary elite, constitutes a cathartic sacrifice, one that can usher humanity into a utopian future either by wiping away its actual past (Marxist-Leninism) or by returning it to a mythical, uncorrupted past (romantic fascism). More people perished through the totalitarian convulsions of the last century—Hitler's Holocaust, Stalin's rampages, Pol Pot's killing fields, Mao's liquidations of entire classes—than were killed in all the wars of any prior century.

The logic of this extremism and its proponents is horrifyingly clear. Transforming a largely resistant world into their own image required unprecedented measures, including the unleashing of unparalleled bloodshed and terror. But that could only happen if the revolutionary vanguard were released from accountability to all known norms and standards of behavior.

Thus, a fourth trait that radical Islamism borrowed from revolutionary Western ideology is the complete elevation of rule of the "ideologically correct" man above rule of law. This involves not just superseding the rule of law inherent in modern democracy, but also ignoring divine law as interpreted by scholars in traditional Islam. Both these systems of law serve as a check against absolute totalitarian power. That is why both have been flouted by the proponents of Islamist extremism, who reserve for themselves the role of ultimate arbiter of right and wrong.

Simply stated, to define one's enemies to include anyone who does not embrace Al Qaeda's views, including hundreds of millions of Muslims, and then treat them as legitimate military targets, is to assert that bin Laden is the ultimate authority on Islam, the Qur'an, and the divine will. This notion, along with its murderous implications, is motivating an increasing number of Muslim clerics and scholars to speak out against bin Laden and Al Qaeda. In 2007, one of Al Qaeda's intellectual architects sent a fax from Tora Prison in Egypt to the London office of the Arabic newspaper *Asharq Al-Awsat* dramatically announcing his defection from its cause. In that letter, Sayyid Imam al-Sharif (known as Dr. Fadl) rejected Al Qaeda's violence as contrary to Islam, adding that "there is a form of obedience that is greater than the obedience accorded to any leader, namely, obedience to God and His Messenger."[8]

Tellingly, Ayman al-Zawahiri, bin Laden's deputy and Al Qaeda's chief planner and ideological theorist, responded by issuing a lengthy "rebuttal" to Dr. Fadl's clearly damaging announcement. Yet it is not only bin Laden and al-Qaeda who embraced a totalitarian vision of absolute power. After he seized control of Iran, Khomeini proceeded to advance the revolutionary doctrine that his was the single, ultimate religious and political authority in that country. In an edict released in 1988, Khomeini claimed that "the government is authorized unilaterally to abolish its lawful accords with the people and . . . to prevent any matter, *be it spiritual or material*, that poses a threat to its interests" (emphasis added). He went on to make the astonishing declaration that "for Islam, the requirements of government supersede every tenet, *including even those of prayer, fasting, and pilgrimage to Mecca*" (emphasis added). Thus did Khomeini subordinate the traditional prescriptions of religion to the absolute dictates of the state.[9]

Like bin Laden, Khomeini was essentially declaring himself and his movement to be above the law, beyond the reach of traditional religious authority. Highlighting this fact were the enormous posters of Khomeini that hung in public places during his reign. This cult of personality is redolent of the historical totalitarian practice of elevating despots to iconic status. Stalin, Hitler, Mao—each elevated himself into the personification of the dominant ideology. Thus was the cult of the supreme, infallible leader on full display.

Clearly, then, the intellectual and political aspects of violent Islamist extremism mirror Western radicalism. This extreme Islamism reflects Western totalitarian ideology thinly cloaked in Muslim rhetoric. But this raises a crucial question. Is it a coincidence? If not, how and when did this foreign, ideologically driven outlook penetrate the Middle East, distort Islamic teaching, and develop into the threat we are facing today?[10]

## History: Tracing Radical Islamism's Western Roots

The answer may be found by examining the decade that followed World War I. For a number of Muslim-reared intellectuals, it was an especially dark and painful chapter of history. The ignominious collapse of the Ottoman Empire and the subsequent assumption of mandate authority over much of the Middle East heartland by Britain and France were viewed as humiliating setbacks to the advance of Islamic civilization. The abolition of the caliphate in 1924 by the Turkish reformer Kemal Ataturk, in the land where proud Ottomans once ruled, was perhaps the crowning indignity of that period.

Post-World War I Germany provides a striking parallel. Like the Ottomans, the Germans lost the war. Many felt humiliated by the defeat and its implications, including the harsh terms of the Treaty of Versailles. It was in the bleak postwar era that Hitler's Nazis blamed Germany's troubles on foreigners and advocated the recovery of a mythical past by empowering a pure Aryan master race that would rule not just Germany but the world. In that same era, in response to a similar sense of crisis, the Muslim Brotherhood was founded in 1928 by Hassan al-Banna, an Egyptian schoolteacher. Blaming his civilization's problems on the rise of foreign influences, Banna favored a similar return to a romantic, idealized origin, so that an ideologically pure pan-Islamist movement and its leaders would arise and its leaders would take their place as masters of the Middle East and eventually the world. University of London professor Efraim Karsh noted how Banna admired Hitler and Mussolini, created a paramilitary wing patterned after Hitler's SS, and synthesized "the tactic of terror, the cult of death, and the lust for conquest."[11] Banna himself stated that "death is an art, and the most exquisite of arts when practiced by the skillful artist."

What Banna supported, in other words, was not only the rejection of liberal democracy, but the violent perversion of traditional Islam for the purpose of advancing a more radical, politically driven vision similar to today's radical Islam. Not surprisingly, Banna warned his followers to expect vehement opposition from traditional Muslim scholars and clerics.[12]

The affinity of his vision with totalitarianism, along with its hatred of Jews and Zionism, led Banna's Brotherhood to connect with Nazi Germany through the Grand Mufti of Jerusalem, Haj Amin al-Husseini, a Nazi collaborator who lived in Berlin for most of the Second World War. The intellectual commerce between Banna's Islamism and Hitler's Nazism helped open the Middle East to paranoid conspiracy theories alleging Jewish capitalist control of the world's financial and economic systems, as well as the notorious Czarist forgery, "The Protocols of the Elders of Zion," about a supposed Jewish plot to control the world. And following the end of World War II, when Britain and the United States were seeking to apprehend Husseini as a war criminal, the Brotherhood helped ensure that he was granted asylum in Egypt.[13]

By the close of World War II, Banna's organization claimed more than 500,000 members in Egypt alone. More important, in the decades that followed, it spawned a new generation of leaders and disciples that created the extremist organizations of today, along with their totalitarian mindset and practices.

In 1949, following the assassination of Egypt's prime minister, the government responded by assassinating Banna. His successor,

Sayyid Qutb, further articulated the Islamist vision, employing both Marxist and fascist critiques of democratic capitalism. Tellingly, he compared his version of Islam not to other religions, but to distinctly secular ideologies and stages. As part of this effort, Qutb explicitly embraced Marx's stages of history. Along with Marx, he believed that just as industrial capitalism had replaced agrarianism, capitalism, in turn, would yield to a superior Marxian socialism. Significantly, he added Islamism as the fourth and final stage that would follow Marxism.[14]

Ultimately, Qutb wanted this extremist ideology imposed from above by an elite revolutionary vanguard seizing state power in Bolshevik fashion. Building on Banna's teachings, he supported unleashing this vanguard in pursuit of a world caliphate by removing all traditional restraints on warfare. In 1966, Qutb, along with a number of other Muslim Brotherhood members, was hanged for conspiring to assassinate Egypt's nationalist president, Gamal Abdel Nasser.

Among the many members arrested in connection with that conspiracy was a fifteen-year-old named Ayman al-Zawahiri.[15] Zawahiri first met bin Laden in the mid-1980s and then joined him in Sudan in the early 1990s. He is said to have exclaimed that bin Laden was "the new Che Guevara."[16] By the early 1980s, bin Laden was in Afghanistan. Concomitantly, in Peshawar, Pakistan, fellow member Sheikh Abdullah Azzam was providing the infrastructure to fight the Soviets through his Office of Services, which would later form the basis for Al Qaeda.[17]

Today, the Muslim Brotherhood publicly renounces violence. Yet unquestionably its early formation and development, influenced heavily by Western totalitarianism, helped produce not only the ideology but eventually the leadership for today's violent Islamist extremism.[18] That includes not only the Sunni extremism of bin Ladenism but the Shiite radicalism of Khomeini's regime in Iran. From the beginning, Banna had envisioned a pan-Islamic ideological and political network that would span the Muslim world.

As World War II drew to a close, Navab Safavi, an Iranian cleric, created a radical group that assassinated a number of Iranian intellectual and political leaders. In 1953, he visited the Brotherhood in Egypt. While Safavi was later executed for attempting to assassinate his country's prime minister, several among his group went on to play critical roles in helping Khomeini seize power a generation later.[19] Khomeini's conversion from conservative cleric to radical Islamic ideologue by the early 1970s helped paved the way for the Revolution of 1978 and for Islamism to penetrate Shiite strongholds in the Middle East, including parts of Lebanon, where the terrorist group Hezbollah was created.

Far from being an exclusively Shi`a phenomenon, Khomeini's revolution made it a point to honor Sunni fellow radicals. Under the ayatollah, a postage stamp commemorating Qutb was unveiled, and under Khomeini's successor, Ali Khamenei, Qutb's voluminous works were translated into Persian.[20] Until 2006, streets in Tehran, such as Islambouli Street, could still be found named in honor of the Sunni assassins of Egyptian President Anwar Sadat, with collages erected in their memory.

## We Are at War

In short, just as totalitarian communism and fascism were the main ideological threats of the twentieth century, the totalitarian ideology of violent extremist Islamism wars against the world today. Based on the words and deeds of the terrorists themselves, we are very much at war. In 1998, Osama bin Laden made an open declaration of war that ended with the command "to kill the Americans and their allies—civilian and military, in any country where it is possible to do it."[21] In the decade following, bin Laden and his cohorts have done precisely that, plotting against the entire global system of security, safety and prosperity.

Their efforts belie the scope of the current struggle. We are at war with an ideology that is every bit as fanatical and ruthless as that of fascism or communism. Spread by a sinister network of cult-like entities that spans the world, this fanatical worldview sanctifies the torture and slaughter of innocents; it denies the dignity and humanity of its opponents; and it includes among those it targets mainstream Muslims who dare to reject its pseudo-religious message of intolerance and bigotry.

These extremists have proved themselves quite capable of waging the war that they have declared. They have been helped in part by twenty-first-century technology, which has provided even small groups with enormous capability for destruction and damage. Radicals affiliated with Al Qaeda or the Taliban or other similar extremist groups—from North Africa to Iraq and South Asia—are fighting for, and sometimes achieving, control of territory that they use to train, assemble advanced weaponry, and perform experiments to develop ever deadlier ways of killing their enemies, and over which they impose their own vision of repressive law and seek to dominate local life.

And finally, through atrocities like the 9/11 bombings, the radicals have demonstrated that they are quite capable of visiting consequences upon us every bit commensurate with war. Their goal is clear; what our enemies want is "a dialogue with bullets and the ideals of assassination, bombing and destruction." These are not my words; they are from an Al Qaeda training manual.

The nature of our enemies and the ideological threat we face brings to mind Winston Churchill's famous dictum, uttered in 1946 in reference to a different threat, that of the Soviet Union, but equally applicable here: "There is nothing they admire so much as strength, and there is nothing for which they have less respect than for weakness."[22] Simply put, this is how ideological fanatics view the world. Whether it is Adolf Hitler or Josef Stalin, Osama bin Laden, or President Mahmoud Ahmadinejad of Iran, for every fanatic, weakness is provocation. That is why we must never fool ourselves into thinking that submissiveness is a path to peace.

The United States has heeded this counsel. Following 9/11, President Bush took decisive action, striking back against Al Qaeda in Afghanistan, deploying our intelligence assets across the globe, capturing or killing terrorists on nearly every continent, and partnering with our allies on shared intelligence against this common menace. Without such steps, the United States would have doubtless faced other, equally devastating attacks over the past eight years.

But there is another element in this struggle that is as important as strength: resolve. In his day, Ronald Reagan counseled that the United States should be "not warlike, not bellicose, not expansionist—but firm and principled in resisting those who would devour territory and put the soul in bondage."[23] Today, we can heed this advice by preventing our foes from attaining two monumental goals that they seek to achieve.

The first is the acquisition of weapons of mass destruction, chief among them nuclear weapons. Simply put, we cannot allow such a capability ever to pass into the hands of a global network of terror. For bin Laden and his fellow travelers are at war, not just with America or the West, but with the values and principles, the habits and institutions of modern civilization. These extremist ideologues aim to destroy the modern world by unleashing the tools of modern technology. Make no mistake: this enemy, if it ever obtains a modern nuclear weapon, has every intention of using it.

The second goal of our ideological foes is to gain possession and control of nation-states. Just like the Nazis before they seized power in Germany or the Marxists before they took over in Russia, our enemies are seeking countries to conquer because they desire platforms from which they can launch other kinds of attacks. As we know, Al Qaeda ran Afghanistan through its surrogate, the Taliban, and that malignant alliance is part of what made 9/11 possible. Today, Islamic radicals seek to recreate such a safe haven in Iraq, Afghanistan, Somalia, and elsewhere. And that is why we must continue to work to ensure that they never acquire those platforms.

We are fighting a battle not only of armaments but of ideas. And therein lies our greatest strength. Our enemies are animated by a fanatical ideology in which prejudice is lionized instead of condemned, and solving disputes through bombings is viewed as the preferred path to achieving consensus. We, on the other hand, believe in the power of reason, the great legacy bequeathed to us by our intellectual ancestors, including the forefathers of this country. In contrast to our enemies, many of them believed that when we look at the world through reason, we are not betraying faith in the Almighty, but are obeying a divine call to pursue knowledge and truth wherever they lead. Through the liberation and exercise of reason, humanity has achieved more in the last three centuries than in all of its history. We have birthed modern science, we have conquered ancient diseases, we have freed people from poverty and starvation, we have triggered the information age, and we have made the world a better and brighter place.

We are heirs to the age of reason, locked in a struggle for hearts and minds over this very matter, a struggle whose outcome might well determine the fate of our civilization and this globe. We dare not walk away from this battle, and we cannot allow fanatics to drag parts of the world into a dark age of ignorance and fear, degradation and servitude, disrespect for women, and prejudice and contempt for those with whom there is disagreement.

We are not in a battle against religion, because, as we have seen in the lives of some of the greatest men and women of our age, there is no necessary conflict between reason and faith. But we are indeed in

34

a fight for our future, and it is this fight to which we must dedicate ourselves.

## Combating the New Totalitarianism

How, then, should the United States combat its current ideological foes?

First, we should encourage more Muslim scholars and clerics to make clear to the world—especially the Muslim world—that extremist Islamism is not Islam, but a politicized perversion. We must also help amplify the voices of scholars and clerics that have already been raised, making sure their message is heard throughout the world

Second, we should make clear that we ourselves understand that radical Islamism is not true Islam because we recognize its poisonous roots only too well, having opposed them in World War II and throughout the Cold War. We must emphasize how these roots can be traced to the West's own backyard, to ideologies that deify the state, threatening mainstream Islam as well as Western democracy. And we must fight radical Islamist ideology as we fought its Western predecessors, with a complete array of tools, including developmental and humanitarian assistance to despairing people and nations that remain vulnerable to the terrorists' message.

Third, as an alternative to this radical tyranny, we should continue our efforts to support democracy and the rule of law throughout the Muslim world and across the globe. In this sense, we must stress that the embrace of democracy, when coupled with respect for rule of law, need not be inimical to Islam. On the contrary, the principle of rule of law squares with Islam's understanding that no reign—including that of the majority—should be absolute because no ruler is divine. Democracy makes room for precedent and tradition, holds rulers accountable, and empowers constructive reform, not destructive revolution. Understood in this way, it can fit with mainstream Islam.

The experience of Muslims in the United States provides a powerful affirmation of this assertion. For generations, Muslims have flourished under democracy in our country. They have practiced their religion freely, expressed their ideas openly, pursued education and careers productively, and passed along their faith to their children successfully. This testifies to the U.S. commitment to honor and respect the adherents of all religions, including Islam, and suggests that the practice of Islam is compatible with the existence of free societies and governments.

Can stable Muslim democracies emerge? They show signs of having emerged in countries like Malaysia and Indonesia. They are struggling to emerge in Iraq and Afghanistan. What we are witnessing might not be Jeffersonian democracy, but it may not have to be. Different cultures can and will produce distinct versions of democratic governance. Time will tell whether democracy will spread.

In the end, if we wish to defeat terrorism, our course is clear. We must confront and expose its demonic ideology, which sacrificed more than 100 million human beings to fascism and Marxism in the last century and demands further sacrifices today. As we do, we can offer a more hopeful vision—one that represents the best and not the worst that our civilization can offer.

# PREVENTION

# Securing the Border—and Reforming Immigration

IMMIGRATION is a source of tremendous strength for our country, but it can also be a source of great division and even confusion for Americans. Talk of immigration tends to stir powerful emotions, provoke strong responses, and generate equal amounts of heat and light in our political discourse.

Most Americans do seem to agree on one thing: they want something done about illegal immigration. They are tired of decades of lip service, inaction, and broken promises. Not surprisingly, they have grown cynical about the federal government's willingness to act. Given the serious threat posed by terrorism in the post-9/11 world, they fear the consequences of perceived inaction at our borders.

In the summer of 2007, Congress stood on the verge of passing comprehensive immigration reform that, for the first time in decades, would have given the federal government new tools and resources to protect the border and our homeland, enforce immigration laws, and create new channels to boost legal migration through temporary worker programs and improved paths to citizenship.[1] The bill's provisions included a measure to bring millions of undocumented workers into a legal, regulated status—provided they pay a fine and go to the back of the line to wait their turn. Proponents of the bill, including the Bush administration, believed this would have solved one of the major challenges of immigration enforcement: combating the economic draw that encourages people to risk life and limb to cross the border. Equally important, it would have freed law enforcement to focus more fully on truly dangerous individuals, including gang members, drug and human traffickers, and potential terrorists.

Unfortunately, the Senate voted down the legislation. Among the key causes for the bill's failure was skepticism that the federal government was serious about securing the border and enforcing the law. Too many years of unchecked illegal migration had created a credibility problem. In the eyes of its detractors, comprehensive immigration reform would only result in further illegal immigration while rewarding those who had already broken the law.

To help restore credibility and create a path for future reform efforts, the administration put forward a set of 26 measures designed to immediately address existing immigration challenges within the scope of current law.[2] The measures contained three central pillars: securing the physical border through additional infrastructure, manpower, and technology; strengthening interior enforcement by targeting dangerous illegal immigrants as well as businesses that violate the law; and improving temporary worker programs and legal immigration.

While none of these steps alone solve the problem of illegal immigration, they have contributed to substantial, measurable progress to turn the tide of illegal immigration into the United States. They also have helped make it clear that the government is taking this challenge seriously. Ideally, this will help clear the path for future reform efforts in Congress.

## Securing the Border

Most of those entering the United States illegally are only seeking a better way of life. The fact that they can enter illegally is, however, a national security vulnerability that must be addressed. Moreover, the manner of crossing—often in the desert heat, and at the mercy of smuggling groups—is a serious humanitarian problem. Additionally, illegal drug smuggling continues to pose a major challenge at the border. In 2008, U.S. Customs and Border Protection (CBP) seized nearly 3 million pounds of illegal narcotics at the border. Most of the drugs that enter our country do not remain at the border. Their ultimate destination is American cities and communities. In a very real sense, what we do to stop drugs at the border protects the interior of our country.

Moreover, areas where drug smugglers and human smugglers are able to operate freely often experience problems with trash, human waste, and abandoned vehicles, which have a damaging impact on wildlife, vegetation, and water quality. Campfires can get out of control and create wildfires, also harming local habitat. Trespassing and even violence affect citizens in surrounding areas.

Finally, after the September 11 attacks, it became clear that dealing with the ease of illegal entry as a national security vulnerability had to assume a new urgency, given the opportunity it posed for those who wanted to launch further strikes on the homeland or commit serious crimes against our citizens. Indeed, over the past year, CBP apprehended more than 200 people with serious criminal records, including convictions for rape, murder, and child molestation. And it continues to encounter individuals seeking to illegally enter the United States from countries with an established nexus to terrorism. To combat these problems, the government is pursing three strategies to secure the southern border: pedestrian and vehicle fencing; additional Border Patrol agents; and new technology.

From the government's perspective, fencing is a valuable tool that makes the job of the Border Patrol easier and more efficient in certain areas. In particular, fencing helps to slow down people who are attempting to dash across the border. This lengthens the amount of time the Border Patrol has to intercept and apprehend migrants before they can vanish into the interior. Fencing also prevents vehicles laden with drugs or illegal immigrants from crossing the border. To the extent that fencing can minimize traffic flows, it also helps protect the natural habitat.[3]

In building the fence, we sought the cooperation of landowners, state and local leaders, and members of border communities. While some will dispute this claim, we literally held hundreds of town hall meetings with property owners and concerned citizens. We were always willing to listen to concerns and take suggestions. In fact, our direct consultation with a local community in Hidalgo County, Texas, led to an agreement to design the fence in a way that meshed with local flood control needs. As a result, the government is producing a sixteen-foot wall at the border that will serve both to protect against possible floods from the Rio Grande and as a very powerful barrier against drug smuggling and human smuggling into Texas. This is a win-win situation.

Ultimately, our rationale for building fencing is to serve the operational needs of the Border Patrol. If fencing will help reduce migrant flows and the entry of drugs in certain areas, then we have a compelling interest to build it. We have to weigh the good of the entire country—which absorbs the impact of smuggling—against the desires of border residents who have economic or political objections.

42

Beyond fencing, we also have dramatically expanded the U.S. Border Patrol, whose job is to intercept, apprehend, and remove people who enter this country illegally, as well as to intercept the flow of illegal drugs and other contraband. The Border Patrol was expanded from approximately 9,000 agents at the beginning of the Bush administration to more than 18,000 agents at the end of 2008. This is the largest expansion in the agency's history.[4] The third element of our strategy is technology. Twenty-first-century tools are needed at the border, which means more than just fencing and barriers. It means high-tech solutions as well, such as unmanned aerial systems and ground-based radar, including systems that allow the Border Patrol to map exactly where migrants are entering so that they can direct their teams to intercept. Technology will never be a substitute for the experience and intuition of well-trained Border Patrol agents, but it helps them be more effective in a challenging border environment.

Are these efforts having an impact on illegal immigration? Perhaps the best statistical measure can be found in the number of apprehensions at the border. Since 2005, Border Patrol apprehensions of illegal migrants attempting to cross the border dropped a full 40 percent, suggesting that fewer people are attempting to enter the country. In 2008, apprehensions dropped 17 percent.[5] Coupled with other third party indicators, including a significant reduction in remittances to Mexico and Latin America, as well as fewer people in traditional staging areas at the border, we are confident that this reflects a significant change in past trends. Further validation can be found in an independent Pew Hispanic Center study, which in October 2008 noted that "from 2005 to 2008, the inflow of immigrants who are undocumented fell below that of immigrants who are legal permanent residents. That reverses a trend that began a decade ago. The turnaround appears to have occurred in 2007."[6] The Pew study found that in 2007, for the first time in years, there was no increase in the net illegal population in the United States. These are encouraging signs for those responsible for protecting the border, suggesting that the policies instituted by the Bush administration can have a positive impact on border security.

## Interior Enforcement

Moving away from the borders, we also have to look at the issue of enforcing the law in the interior. Only by promoting a legal workforce can we reduce the incentives for people to enter the country illegally. As we know, what brings the vast majority of illegal migrants into the United States is the prospect of jobs. When businesses hire illegal immigrants it works against our policy of controlling the border. It also encourages more people to break the law and exposes workers to potential abuse by their employers. Thus, interior enforcement remains a major part of our strategy. Worse, we know that some proportion of the people who enter the United States illegally do not come here to do legitimate work; they come to commit crimes. Our first priority is to identify those in the country illegally who are criminals or gang members and arrest them. To this end, we have expanded both our anti-gang initiatives and our fugitive operations teams.

Since the department's creation in March 2003, the Immigration and Customs Enforcement Agency (ICE) has identified and arrested more than 11,400 illegal alien gang members in the United States,[7] including leaders and affiliates of some of most dangerous transnational gangs in the world, such as MS-13. Taking these individuals off our streets makes our communities safer. We also have added more than 100 fugitive operations teams to locate, arrest, and remove fugitives from justice.[8] In 2008 these teams arrested more than 34,000 individuals.

We also have stepped up our efforts at worksites. This does

not mean randomly going after businesses where we suspect illegal hiring has taken place. Our priority is to identify employers who flagrantly and systematically abuse immigration laws as part of their business model. Our underlying belief is that if a business cannot survive without illegal labor, then perhaps it should not be in business. Beyond targeting egregious violations of the law, we also have started to bring criminal complaints against employers and employees who engage in identity theft and rampant use of fraudulent or stolen Social Security numbers as part of the hiring process.

In May 2008, ICE conducted one of the largest worksite enforcement actions in U.S. history, arresting more than 380 illegal workers at Agriprocessors, Inc., a meat packing company in Postville, Iowa.[9] Ultimately, 305 of those arrested were convicted of criminal offenses including identity theft, false use of a Social Security number, and illegal reentry into the United States. In July, two of the company's supervisors were arrested and charged with crimes that included aiding and abetting aggravated identity theft and encouraging aliens to reside illegally in the United States. One of these supervisors pled guilty to charges of conspiracy to hire illegal aliens and one count of aiding and abetting the hiring of illegal aliens. In October the former CEO of the company was arrested; he faces charges of conspiring to harbor illegal aliens for profit, aiding and abetting document fraud, and aiding and abetting aggravated identity theft.

Of course, the use of a stolen Social Security number to gain employment is not a victimless crime, as some would believe. In many cases, these numbers belong to U.S. citizens who later feel the negative consequences of having their identities stolen—owing taxes on wages they did not earn or suffering persistent credit problems. In all, ICE made more than 5,100 administrative arrests and 1,100 criminal arrests in worksite cases in fiscal year 2008, including bringing criminal charges against 135 employers.[10] By comparison, the agency made 25 criminal arrests in fiscal 2002. This is a significant increase in the size and potency of the sanctions we are bringing against people who deliberately violate our laws against employing illegal aliens.

These efforts are not just about enforcement. In reality, we know that most employers do not want to violate the law. The vast majority wants to comply, which means we must give them the tools to make sure they can. Immigration reform should not just be about sticks. There must be carrots to help people abide by the law. In particular, we need to give employers easy-to-use and accurate tools that allow them to verify that when they hire someone, that person has a lawful right to work in the United States. A major element of our approach has been to expand the E-Verify system.[11] E-Verify, formerly known as Basic Pilot, is a web-based program that allows employers to check electronically whether a worker is authorized to work in the United States by comparing the person's name and Social Security number to ensure they match; 99 percent of legal workers are instantaneously verified by E-Verify. A legal worker who is not verified because of a clerical error is usually able to resolve the issue in less than two days. Of course, some workers will not choose to resolve the mismatch. This is because they are probably here illegally or using a false Social Security number and name. In other words, they are not authorized to work in the United States. More than 96,000 businesses currently use this system, and to date more than six million new hires have been queried. Several states also have enacted laws encouraging or requiring businesses to use the system. In addition, the federal government has proposed a regulation that would require all federal contractors to be checked through E-Verify. If we expect American businesses to use this system, we should set an example by using it ourselves.

## Promoting Legal Migration

But as we press the accelerator on enforcing the law, we do not want to step on the brakes with respect to legal employment. The American economy needs workers, even with recent increases in unemployment. If businesses cannot satisfy our workforce needs at home, they will turn to other countries. We believe that foreign workers should enter our country in a way that is legal, visible, and regulated. This will help protect the wages of American workers. It will help protect illegal workers from harm or exploitation at the hands of their employers. It is good from a security standpoint, because in the twenty-first century we need to know who is in our country and why they are here. And it will dry up what fuels the human smuggling organizations that prey upon those seeking to illegally cross the border. The federal government currently has several programs in place to help fill our economy's workforce needs. We want these programs to be as accessible and attractive as possible so that people will use the current legal pathways. But the reality is that these programs often fall short of expectations or are viewed as too much of a hassle or burden for employers to navigate.

For this reason, the Bush administration proposed amendments to a number of visa programs for seasonal agricultural workers, non-agricultural seasonal workers, highly skilled workers, workers under NAFTA, and immigrant students with degrees in science, technology, engineering, or mathematics who have accepted employment in the United States.[12] For each of these programs, we have sought to streamline application procedures, extend the length of stay for workers, or build more fairness and transparency into the process. In the case of foreign students, we have sought to allow them to continue to work while they await a work visa. This is not only good for them; it creates jobs in the American economy for others as well. Apart from temporary worker programs, we have also taken a rigorous look at our legal immigration process under the U.S. Citizenship and Immigration Services (USCIS). As much as we want to discourage illegal immigration, we want to encourage legal immigration. There is a reason why each year hundreds of thousands of people seek U.S. citizenship. America remains a beacon of hope and freedom and opportunity for people around the world. Indeed, since its creation in 2003, USCIS has naturalized more than three-and-a-half million new Americans, including more than one million in fiscal 2008, a record and one for which our country should be proud.[13] Included in this total are more than 8,200 military personnel serving our country overseas, including in Iraq and Afghanistan.

For those seeking to become U.S. citizens, we have continued to work very hard to modernize outdated business practices and reduce the current backlog of immigration applications, which is a source of frustration for those who have obeyed the rules and waited their turn in line. What we cannot do, however, is sacrifice security in the name of speed or efficiency. We will not award citizenship until an individual has cleared an FBI name check and we are confident that individual is not a national security threat. By the summer of June 2009, 98 percent of all name check requests will be completed within 30 days with the remaining two percent completed in 90 days or less. Clearing this backlog will go a long way toward restoring faith in our legal immigration system and the government's ability to handle increasing application volumes.

## The Road Ahead

None of the steps we are taking will provide a total solution to our nation's immigration challenges. In the end, a truly permanent solution to the problem will require a more comprehensive look at the issue of immigration reform, and that will require Congressional action. Congress will need to create an immigration system that satisfies our nation's economic needs while being humane to those who want to work in our country.

Until that time, the federal government should continue to show the American people that we can uphold our commitments. It is important that the new administration not step away from the path we have taken or reverse direction. We need to continue to show the American people that we can secure our borders, enforce the law, and protect and defend the homeland. If we do that, there will come a time in the future where the public may trust the government to expand temporary immigration. Perhaps then our country will be prepared to open the door to more legal immigration and more temporary workers and once and for all address this long-standing challenge.

# Using Every Tool

IN the battle against its terrorist foes, the United States continues to deploy a wide range of preventive tools and options, ranging from law enforcement to military action. Are they serving us well? If they are, we should continue to build on that success by improving their deployment. One way of assessing their effectiveness is to ask a simple question: are we safer today than we were on 9/11?

When confronting this question, there are two opposite extremes that must be avoided: one, hysteria and fear, and the other, complacency and an almost blithe disregard of the threats we face. "Hysteria" refers to rhetoric of the following sort: "Here we are, eight years after 9/11 and lo and behold, Al Qaeda still exists, Osama bin Laden remains at large, and terrorists continue to plot and commit atrocities in various places. Nothing we have been doing has worked. Everything is a failure. We are no safer now than we were then." Obviously, such statements fail to mention that there have been no 9/11-style strikes on the country since the attacks on the

World Trade Center and Pentagon that fateful morning. This fact can hardly be attributed to sheer luck or coincidence.

The United States is indeed safer today, and the reason is clear. Since 9/11, this nation and its overseas friends and allies have acted decisively to enhance their own security and the security of freedom-loving people across the globe. U.S. armed forces have destroyed Al Qaeda's original headquarters and platform in Afghanistan. The United States has dramatically improved its intelligence capabilities abroad. Moreover, the United States has captured and killed terrorists, both leaders and foot soldiers, on nearly every continent. We have developed exceptionally strong partnerships with allies in sharing information and combining efforts to deal with terrorism. We have built a new Department of Homeland Security to prevent dangerous individuals and items from entering the country and wreaking havoc and destruction on its people.

Today, Al Qaeda no longer has a state sponsor, as it did when the Taliban ruled Afghanistan before September 11. Consequently, Al Qaeda no longer owns or has free reign over an entire country. Much of its original leadership has been brought to justice in one way or another.

Al Qaeda is also losing in Iraq, which General David Petraeus has called the "central front" in the war on terrorism.[1] It is losing in part because the Sunni tribes have rejected the Al Qaeda fighters and their ideology of extremism, instead partnering with the United States in our "surge" against this terrorist death cult.[2] Additionally, Al Qaeda has suffered an overall loss of its reputation, even in the communities it seeks to influence. Its repeated attacks on innocent Muslims have sullied its image across the Islamic world. Its more recent attacks on Algerian schoolchildren resulted in bin Laden's deputy, Ayman al Zawahiri, actually being confronted in an Internet chat by indignant Muslims and challenged to justify the slaughter of these civilians.[3]

Here at home, because of the establishment of the Department of Homeland Security, the United States has greatly increased its ability to keep terrorists and other lethal individuals out of the country. Eight years ago, America did not have the biometric or fingerprinting capability, analytical capacity, secure identity documentation regimen, or manpower it now has at its ports of entry.[4] The same is true regarding America's borders. As we saw in the previous chapter, the nation has dramatically expanded its Border Patrol and has installed new technology and infrastructure, including a border fence, that will further protect the homeland from those seeking to do it harm.[5]

In concert with these efforts, the United States has pushed its security perimeter beyond its borders by working with foreign countries to conduct more analysis and screening overseas. Our country has developed comprehensive security plans and procedures to protect critical infrastructure.[6] It has built nearly two dozen layers of security into its aviation system. It now fuses and shares intelligence at the state, local, and federal levels in a way that was impossible prior to September 11. Finally, it has overhauled the Federal Emergency Management Agency (FEMA), increasing FEMA's ability to deal with national disasters. Taken together, these actions have made the United States a tougher target for terrorists and other violent individuals. The changes do much to explain the failure of America's enemies to carry out another successful attack on the homeland.

Certainly the terrorists' failure is not for lack of trying. Perhaps the most disturbing example of terrorist efforts is the August 2006 airline plot directed at transatlantic flights arriving in North America from the United Kingdom—a plot that, if successful would have had an impact, in scale and in loss of life, comparable to September 11.[7] The plot, however, along with a number of others in recent years, was disrupted.

In short, the notion of a completely vulnerable and unprepared nation facing an unscathed foe is readily refuted by a veritable arsenal of indisputable facts. It is a denial of all we have learned and accomplished these last several years. But it is here that Americans need to make a critical distinction. The fact that the United States is safer does not mean that it is completely safe and the job is done. If Americans believe that they are no longer threatened, they are oblivious to the dynamic nature of the threat and the adaptive capability of the enemy. If we believe that we are completely safe, then we are falling prey to the opposite of hysteria: the peril of complacency.

## The September 10 Mindset

The voice of complacency sounds something like this. Here we are, eight years after 9/11, and because there have been no attacks on our soil, 9/11 must have been some freakish aberration that is unlikely to repeat itself. Al Qaeda's strength has been hyped by the government, which is exaggerating the threat. There are other things to worry about. This problem has gotten boring, and we should move to something else and focus on other elements of the public agenda.

This is clearly a "September 10" mindset. It is an outlook that cannot conceive of a serious and successful attack on American soil. On September 10, 2001, that mindset may have been understandable because a truly momentous assault had yet to occur. It represented a failure to think the unthinkable. But in the post-9/11 world, with the unthinkable having occurred, such a mindset is hard to fathom, let alone justify. Yet in certain circles, the view that the threat is exaggerated has rapidly gained currency. It is precisely this attitude of complacency that led to the tragedy of September 11. In their book, *America Between the Wars*, Derek Chollet and James Goldgeier chronicle U.S. policy between the close of the Cold War and 9/11. Tellingly, the book pins the blame less on any one administration and more on a public mindset that hampered Washington in addressing the gathering storm clouds.[8] Charles Krauthammer ironically described this period as a "holiday from history."[9] In reality, it was a *false* holiday from history.

As a response to the threat the nation faces, complacency is at least as wrongheaded as hysteria. In the words of the National Intelligence Estimate issued in the summer of 2007, the United States "will face a persistent and evolving terrorist threat over the next three years."[10] It is a threat the nation has successfully handled over the past seven years, but because the threat is rapidly evolving, we will fail in the future if we fail to adapt today.

## The Security Toolbox

In the first chapter of this book, I summarized the threats we will likely face in the coming years not only from a revived Al Qaeda, but from organizations ranging from Hezbollah and the FARC to transnational criminal gangs like MS-13, which could take on a more ideological or political coloration in the future.

These and other dangers should spur the United States to reject complacency, replacing it with a firm resolve to confront these evolving threats and adapt to them. They should also encourage the United States to continue to use the tools and approaches that have protected it from further attacks thus far.

Unfortunately, in all too many legal and policy discussions about these tools and approaches, people have tended to divide into two mutually exclusive camps. One camp appears to advocate a military response to every major threat and challenge, while the other insists that the United States and its allies face solely a law enforcement problem. If the years since 9/11 have taught us anything, it is that both approaches are necessary. Indeed, all approaches must be deployed where appropriate. We must use every tool in the security toolbox, and in the coming years we will have to invent a few tools that do not yet exist.

Clearly, the United States must not eschew the military option. The United States could never have inflicted the operational damage that we did on Al Qaeda had we not taken the fight to Afghanistan. At the same time, however, the nation must continue to use non-military or civilian tools and options. Since 9/11, the United States government has deployed intelligence collection capabilities, including interception of communications. It has harnessed its ability to disrupt the flow of finance using some civil law authorities and has used conventional law enforcement tools, particularly in this country. In recent years, we have arrested and successfully prosecuted a number of people, either directly for terrorist acts or for acts that may not have been terrorist in nature but allowed us to incapacitate those for whom there was reason to believe were terrorists. Taken together, these approaches constitute a layered strategy against terrorism: deterring terrorists from entering the country; capturing or killing them in their home base whenever possible; stopping them in the course of their travel; and bringing them to justice once found here or elsewhere in the world.

Although clearly necessary, these measures are insufficient. None of them strike at the root cause of terrorism: an extremist, dictatorial ideology that celebrates death and seeks the complete subjugation of hearts, minds, and nations to its totalitarian vision. The ultimate way to fight the terrorists is to engage them ideologically as well as physically, challenging their destructive and deadly ideas with ideas of freedom and prosperity. We do this by promoting the rule of law, not the rule of man. We do this by advocating democracy, not despotism. We do this by supporting literacy, not ignorance. We do this by empowering people, in the very communities where terrorists seek recruits, to fight back ideologically, unmasking the terrorists as enemies of and strangers to mainstream Islam, the rule of law, and political democracy. In the battle against the terrorist foe, every tool and option belongs on the table. Those who would have us focus on just one to the exclusion of the others, and those who would have us remove any one of these tools, are seriously misguided.

Even so, some argue that deploying the military against Al Qaeda elevates its status. That is what Seth G. Jones and Martin C. Libicki assert in *How Terrorist Groups End*.[11] But to renounce or severely restrict the military option against terrorists is to place ourselves back in the same box we were in before September 11, one that relied exclusively on the traditional tools of law enforcement and the courts. Had the United States failed to add military tools to the mix after 9/11, it could not have brought the 9/11 perpetrators to justice. With an outlaw enemy in control of a rogue state thousands of miles away, none of the traditional criminal justice tools—from obtaining search warrants to issuing indictments to seeking extradition—would have had an ounce of relevance against Al Qaeda in Afghanistan. Al Qaeda would have continued to use Afghanistan as a platform to launch attacks against America.

At the opposite pole are those who have argued that the law enforcement option is outmoded and have insisted that the government operate entirely on a war footing. Remarkably, the *Washington Post* took this position in an editorial *against* the Bush administration in its case against Al Qaeda member and 9/11 plotter Zacarias Moussaoui in 2003.[12] The *Post* argued that by bringing Moussaoui into an American criminal courtroom, the government was repeating the mistakes of the pre-9/11 past, and urged that the government try him before a military tribunal instead. This position was contrary to the *Post*'s initial support for a civilian trial.[13] The *Post* also contradicted itself in a later editorial entitled "A Way Out," in which it abandoned its support for a military tribunal.[14] As for the Bush administration, it stayed the course. Moussaoui was prosecuted in a civilian criminal courtroom and convicted in 2006 for conspiring to kill American citizens as part of the September 11 attacks.

Contrary to what many believe, the approach the United States has taken since 9/11 has not mandated the use of military tools alone. It has used the military in concert with all of the other approaches, including those of law enforcement. In November 2001, as head of the Justice Department's Criminal Division, I testified before Congress and emphasized that the government intended not only to use its military options, but also every law enforcement tool at its disposal, as well as a full array of other tools, in the fight for the freedom and safety of the American people.[15] It is this comprehensive approach that must continue if the United States is to make further headway in the battle to secure the nation. Those who would insist on elevating or scrapping any of these tools, for political or other reasons, are doing a grave disservice to the nation.

I would go further. Even our full, current array of tools is not sufficient to deal with an ever-evolving threat environment. Today we remain locked into a set of legal authorities and processes that were designed for the previous century, a time when the world was neatly divided between nation-states that waged war and individual groups that committed crimes. Given the current ability of non-state actors like Al Qaeda to wage war, we need to make corresponding changes in how we approach this from a legal standpoint.

This question highlights the challenge: What should a free nation do when it finds someone in its midst who is clearly advocating and recruiting for terrorism but has not yet advanced from advocacy to incitement or actual execution of a criminal plan? If that person has entered the country illegally, one obvious answer would be to send him back to his home country. If he cannot be arrested, prosecuted, or otherwise incapacitated, at least he can be removed and deported.

Under contemporary law regarding migration, however, it is not quite that simple. Under that law, the same open advocacy of terrorism that makes one a threat in a host country allows one to argue that he will not be treated fairly in his home country.[16] Once that argument is raised, Western civilization's hands are often tied. The individual cannot be deported, nor can he be held for something he has not yet done. The result is that a person who has no legal right to be in a country and poses a clear danger to its citizens cannot be jailed in that country nor removed from it.

This is no hypothetical case. It happened recently in Great Britain.[17] A radical Islamist Jordanian preacher named Abu Qatada, widely known as an outspoken advocate and supporter of terrorism, was illegally present in the United Kingdom.[18] According to the United Kingdom Special Immigration Appeals Commission, he was "a truly dangerous individual" who was "heavily involved" in terrorist activities associated with Al Qaeda. Even though he was in Great Britain illegally and a danger to the country, British authorities have been unable to deport him to Jordan; indeed, the British Court of Appeals ruled that he could not get a fair trial in Jordan because he was suspected of terrorism.[19] The very fact that he posed a terrorist threat rendered authorities powerless to remove him. This kind of challenge is common across Europe and is something the West must address. Either the rules should be modified to allow immigration authorities to balance the risks facing illegally present terrorism suspects with the risks facing the public, or the law should allow temporary detention of dangerous illegal aliens until they can be safely removed from the country.

In the end, Abu Qatada is the poster child for a key point that must be reiterated: In the battle against terrorism, the challenge of this nation and its democratic allies is not to reduce the number of options or tools we have in this fight, but to expand them. It is my hope that both here and abroad, future administrations will not only continue to retain and deploy the tools we are using now, but will find new options, fashion new approaches, and adapt our system to the dangers ahead. That is how best to make the United States not only *safer*, but ultimately *safe* in this new century.

# Why Soft Power Works

I T is imperative that over the next decade the United States, in concert with its friends and allies, retain every option at its disposal and apply every available tool or strategy where appropriate against the threat posed by Al Qaeda and like-minded organizations. Certainly that includes the effective use of military options when necessary as well as other tools that may reduce the ability of terrorists to carry out attacks. Most important, however, in order to prevent the growth of terrorist groups themselves, the United States must pursue strategies to win nations and peoples to its side. Use of such "soft power"—a term coined by Harvard University professor Joseph Nye—can help the United States and its allies reduce the appeal of terrorist organizations and deter individuals from joining them.

## A Multifaceted Fight Against Terrorists

The use of military action in recent years against the terrorists has included deposing the Taliban in Afghanistan and combating Al Qaeda in Iraq. During this time, the United States and its allies have also acted to frustrate three key enablers of terrorism—communications, finance, and travel. They continue to intercept and disrupt communications and actively work to freeze the assets of groups and individuals that support terrorism. When it comes to travel, the United States employs three key strategies: collecting limited bits of commercial information in order to identify travelers warranting closer scrutiny, screening incoming individuals through biometrics, and building a system of secure travel documentation through the Western Hemisphere Travel Initiative.

Unfortunately, such measures, while necessary, will likely leave the United States short of a lasting victory in safeguarding the country. To prevail, we must not only work hard to prevent terrorists from attacking, but also expend equal effort to prevent people from becoming terrorists in the first place. That requires addressing the two major factors that are driving the growth of terrorism in the twenty-first century: the continued presence of failed political and economic systems in parts of the developing world, and the emergence of violent Islamic extremism as the most visible competing ideology for those mired in that dismal status quo.

## The True Nature of the Fight

Given these two factors, the course ahead should be clear. The United States must fight not only the extremists but the ideology of their extremism. It must stand firmly against malignant ideas that can only cause further poverty, degradation, and hopelessness by turning the clock back centuries. It must offer the alternative ideals of liberty and democracy, ideals which have brought more progress to more people over the past few centuries than in all the prior centuries combined. In other words, as during the Cold War, the situation must be seen as a war against an ideology, a contest of ideas, and a battle for the allegiance of men and women around the world. It is not a struggle that we began; it is, however, one that we must win. The security of the United States and the world depends on it.

## The Soft Power Solution

To stand on the sidelines would be to allow this extremist ideology to win by default. So what must be done to counter it? When proposing an alternative to radical ideology, the use of soft power becomes key. Part of this effort must involve providing immediate humanitarian aid to those who need it the most.

This is not an unfamiliar task for the United States; the nation has done this throughout its history. In December 2004, for example, the United States responded to the series of catastrophic tsunamis that killed more than 225,000 people in Indonesia, India, Thailand, and Sri Lanka. The government acted immediately by committing $350 million in relief funding to meet a wide array of human needs, ranging from food and water and health and sanitation assistance to education and cash-for-work programs. It sent 16,000 sailors and airmen to evacuate the injured and deliver aid to hundreds of thousands of people in the affected countries. According to the Center on Philanthropy at Indiana University, U.S. private tsunami donations—cash and in kind—exceeded.$1.8 billion.[1]

The overwhelming majority of casualties occurred in Indonesia, the world's most populous Muslim country. While Indonesia is a democracy, the forces of Islamist extremism have been trying to gain a foothold, making it an important ideological battleground. In the wake of the tsunami, the reaction of Indonesians to U.S. aid is instructive. Polls conducted by Terror Free Tomorrow, a nonprofit, nonpartisan organization, indicate that 65 percent of Indonesians now harbor attitudes that are "more favorable" to the United States than before its response to the tsunami, with the highest percentage occurring among people under thirty. A separate poll conducted by the Pew Global Attitudes Project in Indonesia reports that nearly 80 percent of Indonesians affirm that the donations gave them a more positive view of the United States.[2]

It is also worth noting that at the same time the United States was extending its hand to Indonesia, Indonesians were turning decisively against the Al Qaeda-allied extremists responsible for the horrific bombings in Bali in 2002 and in Jakarta in 2003 and 2004. As a result, according to the Pew Research Center, support for Osama Bin Laden plummeted and has yet to recover. In 2002, nearly 60 percent of Indonesians supported him. By 2006, only 33 percent had favorable views of Al Qaeda's leader.

Indonesia is but one example of how soft power in the form of practical compassion can influence attitudes and cast this nation in a favorable light compared to its enemies. There can be little doubt that other actions, such as President George W. Bush's $1.2 billion initiative against malaria, and his $15 billion initial commitment to fight HIV/AIDS, have sown seeds in areas like sub-Saharan Africa. This is yet another region where radical Islamists are attempting to capitalize on disaffection with the status quo.

## The Role of Humanitarian Aid Elsewhere

More obvious examples of the potential effectiveness of foreign aid are Iraq and Afghanistan, as well as Pakistan and Lebanon. In Iraq, as in Indonesia, the extremists' reign of terror has turned many of their supporters against al Qaeda and its affiliates. Even many of the Sunnis in Iraq now back the surge, and its continued successes have led to further support for U.S. actions. This virtous cycle is being strengthened by developmental and reconstruction efforts. From business development to local governance, from literacy campaigns to bank reform, from rural development to school construction, the United States is quietly laying the foundation for lasting progress. Iraq remains a volatile place, but this continued work on the ground, especially when contrasted with Al Qaeda's atrocities, can only produce greater good will toward the United States.

Afghanistan also remains volatile, but as in Iraq, the United States has been engaged in building the institutions of civil society, including education, from the ground floor. During the Taliban's reign, girls were locked out of the educational system. With the help of the United States Agency for International Development (USAID), one of the largest girls' schools opened in northern Afghanistan in 2002, enabling 5,000 to attend classes. More than 600 schools have been built or repaired, and textbooks have been distributed to five million students—3.2 million boys and 1.8 million girls.[3]

In Pakistan, the United States has been increasing its investments in primary education and literacy. This not only promotes education, but also creates potential alternatives to the radical madrassas run and funded by extremists who teach hatred and intolerance and condone violence in Islam's name. Though many madrassas—the Arabic term for "schools"—are neither radical nor religious, in a number of regions extremist-oriented ones are the only form of education available. Maintaining the status quo will only ensure radical Islam's dominance over the next generation of Pakistanis by default. Helping Pakistan invest in alternatives is a wise and sensible response.

Finally, in Lebanon, since the 2006 war the U.S. government has pledged $230 million in humanitarian and reconstruction assistance. Lebanon is a democracy that is threatened by Syria from without and by Hezbollah from within. For years, Hezbollah has provided an array of social services to the areas of Lebanon under its sway. By helping Lebanon, the hand of pro-democracy forces is strengthened, potentially challenging Hezbollah's hold over hearts and minds in certain areas.

In each of these instances, the United States is sending an unmistakable message: While extremists routinely slaughter innocent civilians, including fellow Muslims, we help feed, clothe, heal, and educate the neediest among them. This is action that speaks volumes. It is a way of introducing ourselves by offering a real alternative, beyond an unacceptable status quo on the one side and the forces of terror on the other.

## Financial Challenges and Solutions

All this inevitably involves money, of course. While the United States spends tens of billions of dollars in foreign assistance each year, a number of thoughtful observers, including Defense Secretary Robert Gates, make a compelling case for investing more. Gates correctly notes that foreign aid spending is a minute fraction of what the Pentagon spends each year. His point is that foreign aid can be as essential to homeland security as military spending. It helps us fight the ideological battle across the world against our enemies.

Secretary Gates is right, but he would undoubtedly agree that spending more money, while important, is not enough. The money must reach its intended recipients and be used effectively. One way of ensuring this is to provide aid not only to governments but to worthy nonprofit organizations that operate at the community level. These groups often have the grass-roots connections and dedicated core of volunteers that make them excellent providers of humanitarian and developmental assistance and good stewards of aid money. Through its Office of Faith-Based and Community Initiatives, USAID links the United States with such providers across the globe. This allows for more people to be helped in a more effective way by channeling influential soft power directly into towns, cities, and villages in some of the most troubled corners of the world.

## Promoting Freedom, Countering Terrorism

Linking foreign aid to the kinds of economic and political reforms that promote freedom is another path to achieving these goals. President Bush pursued this as a significant priority throughout his presidency, and the United States should continue to institutionalize this policy as comprehensively as possible.

History teaches us that economic and political freedom is the necessary prerequisite to the emergence of peaceful, stable, and prosperous societies. It is dictatorships, not democracies, that typically start wars or force free societies to go to war to protect security and liberty. And it is command-and-control economies, not free market ones, which help perpetuate the poverty and despair that provide Islamic radicalism a potential opening. It is for these reasons that the 9/11 Commission recommended that a national counterterrorism strategy include economic policies that help others attain or maintain freedom. Besides making progress toward freedom a condition for receiving foreign aid, we can also counter extremism and advance security by championing freedom of trade and travel.

In the Western Hemisphere, democratic nations like Colombia are threatened by homegrown terrorist groups like the Revolutionary Armed Forces of Colombia (FARC). Disturbing new evidence suggests the complicity of Colombia's neighbor, Venezuela, and its leader, Hugo Chávez, in helping this lethal organization undermine a duly elected government. The prospect of nation-state involvement in terrorism within our own hemisphere underscores the importance of having a free-trade agreement with Colombia that will enhance the prosperity of both nations, while providing its pro-U.S. government with further resources for its vigorous fight against narcotic traffickers allied with FARC.

When it comes to freedom of travel, there is no question that welcoming visitors to our country is a concrete way of improving others' perception of the United States. According to a 2007 Pew survey, people who have visited the United States have a decidedly more positive opinion of the country than those who have not. That is why travel policies regarding homeland security—passenger name record data collection, fingerprinting, and secure travel documentation—must continue to be designed in a way that does not impede the flow of legitimate visitors. And it is also why the Department of Homeland Security has signed agreements with such nations as the Czech Republic, Slovakia, Estonia, Lithuania, Latvia, Hungary, Malta, and South Korea, enabling them to become full participants in the U.S. Visa Waiver Program. Their citizens are allowed in the United States for up to 90 days without a visa if they have valid passports. The logic is simple: in order to garner greater support for the country and for its battle against terror and tyranny, the United States must not only keep sending Americans into the world; it must also continue inviting the world to America.

## The Balance of Hard Power and Soft Power

Though perhaps surprising, hard power can actually play a part in advancing the efforts of soft power. Countless Muslims would like to support our endeavors but want to know that we are committed to staying the course before taking that step. That is perfectly understandable, given the threats some of them would face from extremists by taking a bold stand. In Iraq, for example, there is no way the Sunnis would have taken a decisive stand against Al Qaeda's depredations without the commencement and execution of the surge.

When the United States ended Taliban control of Afghanistan, deposed Saddam Hussein in Iraq, and proved willing to stand up to Al Qaeda around the world, countless Muslims were persuaded that the United States was committed to a policy that rejects both the hated status quo and the terrorists' grisly alternative. Many of them are now speaking out for a third way of freedom and tolerance. They are using the technology of the Internet to proclaim their message while countering that of the terrorists and of nations like Iran and Syria which support them. So in a very real way, applying the right kind of hard power can help achieve some of the critical aims of soft power.

## Words May Speak Just as Loudly as Actions

One final point needs to be made about the use of soft power: In the battle of ideas, words matter. Good deeds, while crucial, are not enough. Actions can speak more loudly than words, but it would be sheer folly to neglect the power of words to explain our actions and defend our message. A large part of the world has been subjected for years, if not decades, to a steady drumbeat of extremist propaganda. Policymakers must do a better job in countering its distorted narrative by telling the story of a nation whose founding document declares that freedom and hope are not for a privileged few, but for the whole of humanity.

Moreover, mainstream Muslims, including their leaders, must be encouraged to work among their own communities to rebut the false picture of Islam being propagated by violent extremists who seek to hijack it for their own ideological and political ends. By telling this story and living it before the world, and by combining it with a steely resolve to defend the free world and its values, we can and will see the ideology of terrorism defeated and our world made safer and freer.

# Why Washington
# Won't Work

L ONG before the nation's current financial woes emerged, I was
sometimes asked the kinds of questions that may be summed up
by the query, "Why doesn't Washington work?"

Even back then, this question revealed a widespread perception
that the people who serve in government are either unable or unwilling to get important things done for the country. To the extent that
this perception ignores the good that government routinely does
each day, it is a distorted portrait of reality. Nonetheless, there are
enough glaring examples of government not doing its job well to
lend plausibility to this assertion. Consequently, the question deserves a sober and thoughtful response.

I want to address that response from the perspective of homeland
security. A good place to begin is with a related question posed by
the 9/11 Commission: Why didn't Washington do more in the 1990s

to secure the homeland and prevent the September 11th attacks? This question assumes two things. First, it presumes that in the 1990s the U.S. government was at least generally aware of the threat that terrorism posed to the country. Second, it assumes that, in spite of this awareness, government officials chose to do nothing.

The first of these assumptions is correct. As early as July 1995, a National Intelligence Estimate predicted future terrorist attacks in the United States, and specifically warned that this danger would increase in the very near future.[1] Three years later, in 1998, Osama bin Laden himself delivered a crystal-clear warning. He publicly declared war on America, calling on his supporters to attack not only our military but our civilians wherever they could be found.[2] And he made good on his threat with the bombings of our two embassies in East Africa that same year, and two years later, with the bombing of the USS *Cole*.[3] In 1999, Phase I of the report of the Hart-Rudman Task Force on Homeland Security warned that "America will become increasingly vulnerable to hostile attack on our homeland." The report went on to say, "Americans will likely die on American soil, possibly in large numbers."[4]

Not only was the nation repeatedly warned of a future attack on its soil; a month after President Bill Clinton was inaugurated, and more than eight-and-a-half years before 9/11, the United States actually was attacked on its soil with the first World Trade Center bombing. Two years later, in 1995, the Murrah Federal Building in Oklahoma City was destroyed by a homegrown radical named Timothy McVeigh. During that time, America averted a catastrophic attack on the Lincoln and Holland Tunnels in New York City by adherents to the "blind sheikh," Omar Abdul Rahman.[5] Finally, at the dawn of the new millennium, the nation was spared from a serious attack on the West Coast, thanks to the quick thinking of an alert Border Patrol agent who intercepted a militant named Ahmed Ressam.[6]

While it is certainly true, then, that the United States received general strategic warning about the threat of an attack on its soil, is it accurate to claim that government ignored the risk? No. There were efforts made before September 11, 2001, but tellingly, they were aborted before fruition. Two examples of this failed effort are instructive.

During the 1990s, those focused on the terrorism threat were particularly concerned that dangerous individuals could arrive by exploiting student visas. In 1996, Congress appropriately responded by requiring the creation of a system to track students from countries designated as state sponsors of terrorism (the Illegal Immigration Reform and Immigrant Responsibility Act of 1996, IIRIRA). Sadly, this action prompted an immediate negative reaction from the higher educational establishment, which feared its "business" would be harmed if there were reduced enrollment by foreign students. As a result of pressure from these educational interests, Congress refused to provide the funding to move the program forward.

Thus, when some of the September 11 hijackers began entering the United States in 2000 to attend flight school, we did not have the recommended national student-tracking system. Had there been one, the United States could have discovered that Mohammed Atta had made false statements about his student status, and then denied him entry.

The second example of failure concerned an initiative also proposed in 1996—now called US-VISIT.[7] That proposal required fingerprinting and tracking all visitors to the United States. Fingerprinting and tracking would enable the government to identify visitors illegally overstaying their visas. That year, Congress required the attorney general to develop an automated entry-exit program to collect records on every arriving and departing visitor.

Again this security proposal created a firestorm of opposition. This time, the opposition was mounted by leaders of communities bordering Canada and Mexico. They were concerned that delays or inconvenience would reduce the number of visitors, thus harming border business interests. They lobbied key members of Congress and succeeded in limiting the law to a less-than-fully-deployed entry system. As a result, immigration authorities had no way of knowing whether any of the 9/11 hijackers had overstayed their visas, or tracking how often they traveled inside or outside the country.

These are but two examples of how sensible homeland security initiatives were thwarted by interest group pressure in the pre-9/11 era. Even more important to ponder are the kinds of security measures that no one dared to propose for fear of provoking similar opposition from interested parties.

The easiest way of seeing this is by way of a thought experiment. Let us presume that in early 2000, following all the warnings through word and deed, the U.S. government proposed what the country now has in the post-9/11 world: a Transportation Security Administration taking concrete steps to reduce risk. It would require air travelers in the United States to remove their shoes and submit to a fairly rigorous search, and would create watch lists and require secure travel identification. At that time, any similar proposal would have gone nowhere and been laughed out of the court of public opinion.

Clearly, policymakers faced serious resistance before 9/11 in countering the unmistakable dangers looming on the horizon. And these are not just the effect of individual personalities. Rather, they reflect structural obstacles to taking action. These obstacles are embedded in our political system and operate no matter which party or administration is in power.

Simply stated, what often happens in government, starting with Washington, is that measures designed to promote the general good of the country are countered by small but highly concentrated, well-organized activist groups that perceive their own individual interests to be adversely affected by new proposals or ideas. To be sure, it is everyone's constitutional right to petition or lobby the government and it should come as no surprise when that right is exercised. But it is this structural barrier to progress that explains why more wasn't done to protect America before 9/11 and answers the original question, "Why doesn't Washington work?"

## The First Steps After 9/11

The horror of September 11, of course, appeared initially to have changed everything. America went from imagining a high-consequence terrorist attack to experiencing one. It served as a gigantic wakeup call across our society.

In the immediate aftermath of that national calamity, structural obstacles fell as the United States took vigorous and dramatic steps that previously would have been unacceptable, if not unthinkable. The United States attacked and destroyed Al Qaeda headquarters in Afghanistan. It deployed intelligence assets around the globe. The government fused previously separate intelligence "stovepipes" to allow real sharing of information between some overseas and domestic agencies.[8] Numerous measures were put into effect relating to potential threats to the homeland, from strengthening chemical plant and transportation security to creating watch lists. Congress established the Department of Homeland Security. And DHS built a strong student-tracking system and a fully deployed fingerprinting system for entrants to the nation.[9]

These major steps produced results. While America's overseas allies have been repeatedly attacked, and while the United States narrowly eluded further attack thanks to the disruption of the London airliner plot in 2006, there have been no successful 9/11-style follow-up strikes on the homeland. Unfortunately, the predictable—yet perverse—result of success is that it has fostered the kind of complacency that enables structural obstacles to begin reasserting themselves. We seem to be turning back to business as usual, the way things were before 9/11.

There are several examples. One concerns border security. The vast majority of Americans understand that unrestricted borders encourage not only illegal migration, but the easy flow of drugs, criminals, and potentially terrorists into the country. That is why Congress mandated a series of steps (the Secure Fence Act of 2006), to secure the border, including building fencing where appropriate. While construction has since proceeded, affected landowners have tried to halt its progress. Some fear the fence might harm their enjoyment of property. Others believe it will send a hostile signal to their trading partners across the border. Still others insist it will inhibit the ability of their cattle to get to the Rio Grande..

Understandably, these property owners would prefer not to be inconvenienced. Envisioning costs and consequences that may harm them individually, they agitate politically or file lawsuits to block further construction. But just as the landowners have a perceived interest, so does the rest of America. And while border residents are focused on the burdens of building a border fence, Americans must focus on the cost of not building one. We see the cost, for example, in the form of illegal narcotics flooding the rest of the country. These drugs may not be sold near the border, so the landowners may be unaffected. They will be sold, however, in places like Chicago, New York, or Washington. Thus for their sake, building the fence serves a greater good.

Put another way, the problem is that the beneficiaries of a border fence are widely distributed across the nation and do not see the direct benefit to them as vividly as the opponents see the costs. Those who oppose the fence are far less numerous, but far more concentrated and committed.

A second example of the reassertion of structural obstacles against sensible homeland security measures concerns the issue of secure travel documentation. As the 9/11 Commission asserted, when in the hands of terrorists, travel documentation becomes a form of weaponry.[10] Terrorists had used phony identification to board airplanes and maintain themselves in the United States. Time and again, the ability to obtain fraudulent documents has been a critical element in the planning of terrorists who seek to enter an area in order to carry out an attack.

That is precisely why Congress, in line with the 9/11 Commission recommendations, mandated that we institute measures that tighten travel document security at the borders with the Border Security Act of 2002. One of our measures was designed to reduce number of acceptable forms of travel documentation. At one point, 8,000 different types of documents were accepted for crossing a land border into the United States. That included everything from foreign baptismal certificates to library cards. Another measure was designed to end the practice of letting people cross borders in heavily trafficked areas after merely declaring that they were American citizens.

As with the case of fencing, these security measures have been met by structural obstacles in the form of border businesses concerned about their potential effect on cross-border commerce. These economic interests helped launch a vigorous public campaign to delay our ability to implement the full measure of what Congress mandated on secure documentation.

Again, the problem is the return of business as usual. On the one hand, we see the presence of powerful opposition from small but highly concentrated, well-organized, and directly affected groups near the border. On the other hand, we witness the absence of countervailing intensity from the nation as a whole. It has been more than seven years since September 11, and America has yet to experience the horrific potential consequences of insecure travel identification. There have been no instances of individuals crossing from Canada or Mexico and committing a terrorist attack. Ironically, it is our very success that sows the seeds of potential failure by breeding complacency.

A third example of how structural obstacles in the form of special interests combat the needs of homeland security pertains to the nation's chemical industry. Following a long struggle, Congress agreed to authorize the Department of Homeland Security to set performance-based standards for that industry under the Chemical Facility Anti-Terrorism Act of 2006. The aim was to get companies to dispose of chemical plants using hazardous materials in populated areas, describe attendant risks, and take action to secure themselves against the threat of attacks. One such material is propane, which could become a bomb in place. Indeed, our troops in Iraq have faced the problem of propane bombs.

But when DHS required that companies with large quantities of propane examine their security, the propane industry filed suit against DHS because it did not want to pay the increased costs that would result. The suit failed, but the point remains that in its attempts to advance the common good, government faces continued challenges from intensely interested groups that have the means and motivation to make their stand.

In its attempts to assert the common good against the special pleadings of these groups, government is further hampered by the operation of three critical factors.

The first is what I call anecdotalism. It is the all-too-human tendency to form a policy opinion based on isolated stories rather than the complete picture. The result is a kind of Gresham's Law for government, where a single heart-wrenching story, repeated endlessly across the media, can drive out a policy idea that makes perfect sense for the nation as a whole.

In the area of travel documentation, for example, the case for secure identification is self-evident. It is in the country's interest to know who is trying to come here. Yet from time to time, due either to human error or some other misadventure, somebody has a bad experience at the border with a document. That single story is used to make the case that the country's border security measures are too draconian and must be scaled back. This usually becomes a recipe for maintaining the status quo. The problem is clear. If the goal is advancing the greater good, one cannot govern by anecdotes, no matter how emotionally compelling.

The second factor that strengthens or gives rise to structural obstacles against successful governance is parochialism, or the phenomenon known as NIMBY—"not in my backyard." Indeed, much of the opposition to our security measures is driven by this tendency to put concerns about one's own home or land above the interests of the entire homeland.

A classic example involves border security, where an individual opposed DHS not for putting a fence or camera on his property, but for putting it on someone else's land, allegedly causing illegal border crossers to come through his land. He wanted the fence torn down on his neighbor's property so the border crossers would resume bothering the neighbor, not him.

The third factor that aids the forces of structural opposition to the national interest is what might be called "short-term-ism," an unwillingness to pay a short-term cost in order to achieve a vastly greater long-term benefit. Howard Kunreuther of the University of Pennsylvania has coined an apt acronym for this phenomenon as applied to elected officials: NIMTOF—"not in my term of office."[11] Clearly, legislators and others who run for office are rarely willing to pay costs or incur sacrifices if the expected benefits may not be visible until a generation or more later, when they are no longer holding office and thus unlikely to receive the credit.

A prime example concerns New Orleans and Hurricane Katrina. The impetus for the major damage to the city of New Orleans was the failure of a levee wall on the 17th Street Canal.[12] Clearly, there were structural problems with how the wall had been built. But when I was in New Orleans in 2008, and went to the Canal, I saw that there was a giant barrier in place. That barrier allows the Army Corps of Engineers to drop a massive steel gate that prevents surging water from entering the canal and causing the wall to collapse as it did three years ago.[13]

The obvious question is why this barrier wasn't in place years ago. Had it been, then when Katrina came, the Corps would have dropped the gate, and an enormous amount of devastation could have been averted. In fact, a decade ago, the Army Corps of Engineers proposed precisely that at the canal. It was vociferously opposed by local residents who felt it would spoil their view of the lake, and by environmental groups concerned about its effect on the area's ecology.

## Buying Down Risk

This way of thinking contrasts sharply with the world of homeland security. As everyone who works to protect the United States can attest, a triumph is a term in which nothing happens now. We invest considerable resources in preventing disaster or mitigating risk, but the positive results are either never seen publicly, because we have prevented disasters from happening, or if something does happen after we have left government, our successors will benefit from the hard work and preparedness we have engaged in today.

This is the concept of buying down risk--the idea that one must be willing to incur short-term costs for the sake of long-term benefits, something every homeowner knows. Homeowners must be prepared to invest in a certain amount of maintenance each year in order to reduce the risk of needing costly repairs or having dangerous situations developing in later years.

That is what ownership means. It means accepting the consequences, long term and short term, and managing risk by taking ownership of all of them. The challenge is that we need to own the consequences across government. Clearly, if government is to do a better job in every arena, confronting anecdotalism, NIMBY, and NIMTOF is essential.

The way to combat anecdotalism is by citing contrary anecdotes. It seems that only when we crystallize a problem around an individual circumstance can we ensure the kind of emotional commitment that inspires people on every level to make the necessary and prudent investments to secure the nation. That is why frank discussion about past terrorist attacks is not, as some would claim, fear-mongering. Rather, it is a necessary antidote to the inertia that arises when individuals do not want to be inconvenienced by the short-term impact of policies or programs that prevent further attacks from occurring.

The way to fight parochialism or the NIMBY mentality is to keep asking these simple questions: Is it fair to require that nearly 300 million Americans bear the risk of dangerous people or items coming into the country, simply because the people who happen to be at the border don't want to take certain measures in their backyard in order to protect the whole country? And is it right to ask the brave men and women of our armed forces to keep rendering personal sacrifices for us overseas if we are unwilling to render far more modest sacrifices for the sake of our own security at home? Countering the NIMTOF issue is harder, because it requires society to consider the interests of the next generation, even when they seem to conflict with those of people and groups who are living today.

Regarding all three of these factors, and the larger issue of structural obstacles, the future depends in part on having individuals in government, especially in leadership positions, who are ready, willing, and able to push back vigorously but intelligently. Leaders on every level must be willing to take the initiative on behalf of the greater good, being active decision-makers rather than trying to please everyone or passively mediating among the various interest groups. Moreover, they must not dissipate their energies by trying to fight and win every battle, but concentrate their efforts on the things that matter the most. And once they choose to take their stand and fight the battles that truly matter, they must be willing to endure the slings and arrows of intense and seemingly unrelenting opposition.

In the final analysis, structural obstacles, like death and taxes, are undoubtedly here to stay. They cannot be conquered, but with strong and determined leadership, they can be countered. Washington, or for that matter, government at every level, will always fall short of our deepest ideals and expectations. But progress, not perfection, is still possible, and worth working for.

# *PROTECTION: REDUCING VULNERABILITIES*

# Protecting and Preserving Infrastructure

O NE of the most urgent tasks before the Department of Homeland Security is the continued protection of the nation's critical
infrastructure. Since government's principal function is to protect
the nation, it has a vital role to play. But what kind of role should
this entail? Broadly speaking, there are two possible answers to this
question. The first is what might be deemed the government-alone
answer. This approach calls for businesses that operate infrastructure to be intensively managed by officials in Washington, D.C., or
state capitals. Those who endorse this view hold that the best way
to reduce vulnerabilities is by placing government hands on all the
control levers. They also believe that an optimal strategy for countering threats is to put "boots on the ground" to guard facilities. With
heavy concentrations of uniformed guards and detailed mandates
imposed from the top down, this approach hearkens back to the clas-

sic command-and-control model from the twentieth century. A number of people in Washington would like government to apply this philosophy to homeland security challenges. When it comes to cargo security, for example, they want Customs and Border Protection officers overseas to physically inspect every shipping container before it is sent to America. If we refrain from doing so, they argue, we are being dangerously lax in guarding against impending threats.

DHS has largely rejected this approach for a number of reasons. First, it is often based on the chimerical strategy of risk elimination. Eliminating every risk to the country's infrastructure is impossible. If implemented, the kinds of security measures required to pursue such a strategy could destroy what we are trying to protect, namely, the normal, daily commerce of the United States. If our officers physically inspected every piece of inbound cargo, it could grind commerce to a halt, effectively handing the terrorists the victory they desire. A second reason to avoid such a strategy is the fact that the federal government does not have the financial resources to shoulder 100 percent of America's homeland security responsibilities. It is beyond Washington's means to assume the burden of micromanaging every critical business activity in the United States or supplying sufficient personnel to guarantee a reduction in the vulnerabilities of these activities. Third, DHS rejected this strategy because those who own and operate businesses have a natural incentive to protect them. Owners and operators are normally cognizant of the risks they face, including security threats. They do not need to be told that if a flood or cyber attack destroys their computer system, they might be out of business.

Consequently, rather than pursuing the government-only approach, DHS favors a strategy that treats the business community as an equal partner in strengthening its security. We want to hold businesses accountable, but not micromanage them. This partnership model allows businesses to engage in the familiar task of risk management—creating security measures and channeling resources where the need is greatest—rather than being compelled to pursue the quixotic goal of risk elimination. Such a strategy seeks to have businesses share in the burden of security enhancement. Instead of requiring commercial enterprises to provide a greater degree of protection for assets they already value, this approach affords them the ability to design and implement systems that reduce vulnerabilities, while simultaneously providing the security information and guidance required, as well as the standards and metrics allowing evaluation of progress. The objective is to leverage private-sector capabilities and incentives with federal knowhow in an effort to achieve maximum risk reduction based on the most efficient use of resources.

## Applying the Partnership

Three prominent examples provide a glimpse of how this twenty-first-century partnership can be successful. The first involves a set of chemical security regulations that Congress authorized the Department of Homeland Security to issue. They were issued in response to an obvious vulnerability at certain chemical facilities located in high-population areas, facilities that terrorists might exploit, resulting in the catastrophic release of chemical agents.

In addressing this problem, the department realized that the government-only solution was totally unrealistic. Placing guards at every chemical plant on a 24/7 basis while saddling the industry with a one-size-fits-all mandate would be prohibitively expensive to the government and the chemical firms. Such a strategy would actually risk irreparable damage to the very industry DHS was attempting to protect. As an alternative to this strategy, DHS chose the partnership model. Working with Congress, industry, stakeholders, and academics, the department developed a framework that focused on high-risk facilities, those with the most dangerous chemicals and surrounded by vulnerable population centers. DHS then established a hierarchy of risk. The facilities at greatest risk were in the top tier, while those facing lesser threats were ranked based on an analysis of their vulnerabilities and communities. Based upon the degree of risk, DHS directed companies to achieve specific performance measures. They were required to complete and submit security vulnerability assessments if they were in the high-risk category, develop site security plans, and implement risk-based measures that supported the performance standards. Essentially, the department was setting benchmarks that specified outcomes while permitting businesses to determine the most cost-effective strategies to fulfill them. It was a partnership, utilizing accountability, not bureaucracy. Those who might believe this approach was all carrot and no stick would be incorrect. Companies had the right to decide how to reach the security goals outlined; those falling short were subject to penalties that included fines of up to $25,000 a day. This partnership model resulted in a realistic and workable security solution for the chemical industry. It established clear, achievable security requirements while permitting the responsible companies to find the best way to meet the goals outlined and penalized only those companies that failed to take appropriate action.

A second example of the partnership model may be found in the SAFETY Act, the Support Anti-Terrorism by Fostering Effective Technologies Act of 2002. With Congress's help, DHS formalized liability protections for providers of goods and services designated by the Office of the Secretary of Homeland Security as "qualified anti-terrorism technologies," meaning technologies deemed critical to public safety and security. A key purpose was to remove an obvious roadblock to developing cutting-edge security solutions by limiting the exposure of companies to unnecessary and costly liability suits alleging product malfunctions during an attack.

The third and perhaps most comprehensive application of the model involved the implementation of the National Infrastructure Protection Plan. In unprecedented fashion, DHS brought together federal, state, and local governments in a partnership with the private sector to identify the nation's most critical infrastructure, from key bridges and power grids to levees and cyber systems. Rather than establishing one master plan, this model is actually a collection of 18 plans, each headed by a council, and each tailored to the needs and conditions of a specific sector of the economy. By means of interaction with the sector councils, DHS gets the best security ideas from the private sector while providing relevant information and intelligence. The goal is to achieve maximum advantage in protecting each of these sectors. In developing this plan, the department created a comprehensive list of nearly 3,000 national assets, systems, and networks across the 18 sectors. As a result, when there is a hurricane in the Gulf of Mexico or a series of wildfires on the West Coast, responding agencies know exactly what has to be protected or restored. The agencies also know what alternative mechanisms have to be used while a particular piece of infrastructure is out of commission. This visibility and the ability to go directly to economic and business actors have reduced the impact of disasters that otherwise might have cascaded across the country, affecting the nation's health, safety, security, and economic well-being.

## International and Domestic Initiatives

DHS is conducting a focused survey of infrastructure and vulnerabilities not just at home but also abroad through the Critical Foreign Dependencies Initiative launched in 2007. The initiative identified those elements of critical infrastructure outside of the country that are closely intertwined with domestic industries. We now know, for example, the impact on America's energy environment if a refinery or natural gas field shuts down somewhere in the world, if the electric grid fails in Canada, or if the cyber cables that route traffic between the United States and the European Union incur damage. By identifying and focusing on foreign assets and systems on which Americans are dependent, the government achieves two objectives. First, it can plan for the possibility of disruption. Second, it can help foreign partners and companies protect infrastructure. In short, the partnership approach remains a sound and sensible means of securing the lion's share of U.S. and international infrastructure.

Yet there are unavoidable instances in which government has a much broader and deeper responsibility. The first instance concerns "common goods," meaning infrastructure that is publicly owned and managed, serving wider interests beyond a particular manufacturer or business. This category includes bridges, highways, and levees—infrastructure that protects entire communities and is owned and operated by some level of government, whether local, state, or federal. In these cases, the government is required to assume full responsibility for ensuring adequate protection. A second area involves infrastructure that is controlled by the private sector but is critical to other businesses and a major segment of the population. For example, companies focused on energy transmission are obligated not only to ensure that they are protecting their assets and employees, but to recognize that failure to do so will have a cascading effect on other businesses and people. When it comes to securing this privately owned but publicly indispensable infrastructure, government needs to play a greater role. Because the consequences of failure are so dire and the cascading effects so potentially diverse, an expanded role for government is imperative. These strategies continue to serve the United States well in protecting its infrastructure from terrorism. Regrettably, the nation has not been as successful in protecting these vital assets against simple wear and tear and Mother Nature. Time and again, the appropriate agencies have failed to make the necessary long-term investments required to maintain critical structures against the physical ravages of time or protect them against natural disasters endemic to specific geographic areas.

Simply stated, the United States has not invested enough in the long-term maintenance of its levees, dams, and power grids. As a result of this neglect, the nation spends an inordinate amount of money repairing this infrastructure when it fails. When failure occurs, exponentially larger sums are required for response, relief, recovery, and rebuilding, all caused by an emergency that did not need to happen had government pursued a disciplined plan of regular infrastructure investment. Three prominent examples of governmental failure come to mind. The first is associated with the levee system in Sacramento, California, one of the top at-risk urban areas of the country for flooding. This area of California has experienced five record floods over the past half-century. A major failure of levees in Sacramento would have a disastrous impact on the city's population and could potentially affect much of California. Imagine the consequences of such a failure; a considerable part of America's most populous state would be without water for drinking and agriculture. Yet for decades, what has stood between California and this apocalyptic scenario is a patchwork system of aging levees built more than a century ago when the area was sparsely populated farmland. When the system was first constructed, if the levees were breached, the worst that could happen would be a flooded field. Today, with the area teeming with homes, people, and businesses, a great deal more is at risk. Sacramento is faced with a situation where the heightened risk of flooding, inadequate levee maintenance, and rapid development have all come together to create a recipe for disaster.

To his credit, California Governor Arnold Schwarzenegger has attempted to confront the problem. He has worked with the Federal Emergency Management Agency, U.S. Army Corps of Engineers, and local emergency agencies to address the problem. In February 2006, the governor declared a state of emergency and authorized immediate repair work. These stop-gap measures were followed by a $4 billion bond plan designed to fund levee repairs and flood control projects. Beginning in 2007, DHS partnered with California to conduct a comprehensive review of the state's water system. The department has also worked with the Corps of Engineers on maps depicting where floodplains are located, so that appropriate restrictions on development can be instituted. Unfortunately, these precautions triggered intense opposition from officials and businesses associated with local development. Recent articles in regional newspapers have underscored how county and local officials complained about the new flood maps and the requirement for elevated construction in flood zones. The officials fear a residential or commercial building moratorium could result while new levees are being constructed. This unwillingness to delay economic benefit puts the entire population of this highly developed area at risk. It means that if a levee collapse were imminent, the consequences might be far graver than if prudent measures were expeditiously instituted to reduce the risk of flooding.

A second example concerns New Orleans and Hurricane Katrina. As noted in the previous chapter, the cause of most of the damage to the city of New Orleans was the failure of a levee wall located at the 17th Street Canal. As the water in Lake Pontchartrain rushed back to the southern bank, it put an enormous amount of pressure on the canal that cuts through the city at 17th Street. The canal functioned as a funnel. Water surged into the canal, creating enormous hydraulic pressure, and the levee walls failed. Because of that failure a greater part of New Orleans filled like a bathtub.

Clearly, there were structural problems with how the levee was constructed. I was recently in New Orleans and examined the giant barrier that is now in place at the point where the canal meets the lake. The barrier allows the Army Corps of Engineers, if there is a sudden rise in the lake or a surge, to drop a massive steel gate that would hold back water entering the canal, preventing the kind of hydraulic pressure that caused the collapse of the levee wall four years ago. The obvious question is why this barrier or a similar mechanism wasn't in place a decade ago. If it had been, then when Katrina hit, engineers would have taken immediate action and there would not have been a surge into the canal, the levee wall would not have failed, and the enormous loss of life and economic damage would have been averted. In fact, more than a decade ago, the Army Corps of Engineers proposed such a gate for the 17th Street Canal. It was vociferously opposed by local residents who felt it would spoil their view of the lake and by environmental groups concerned about effects on the area's ecology.

## Private Enterprises and Communities

The Sacramento and New Orleans levees are examples of institutional failure to protect publicly owned resources and infrastructure. The nation should also examine this issue as it applies to privately owned enterprises upon which communities depend. Prime examples are the power and energy grids throughout America. Clearly, once a disaster occurs, restoring power becomes critical. Without power, communities cannot deliver resources, evacuate people, or begin to rebuild. Almost every act depends on the ability to provide energy as rapidly as possible to the affected area.

This emphasis on the role of the private sector includes gasoline stations that provide the fuel that permits residents to get to the grocery store and other locations for necessities. When these facilities are unable to dispense fuel because of a lack of power, recovery efforts stall. This was a major problem in 2005 during Hurricanes Rita and Wilma. That year, Secretary of Energy Samuel Bodman and I wrote to the oil companies to suggest that they install generators at service stations. We outlined how critical these facilities were. Because of communities' reliance on service stations, the owners of these facilities have a responsibility to ensure that they can recover from the damage created by these disasters as quickly as possible. Unfortunately, the overall response to our initiative proved uneven at best. The state of Florida did pass a law requiring gas stations to have generators. But many other states failed to follow suit, and many companies have yet to provide their retail outlets with the capability to resume operation following a disaster.

From each of these examples, the same challenge emerges: Given the continuing problem of a crumbling or vulnerable infrastructure, how can government best ensure the infrastructure's protection and maintenance when faced with powerful and narrowly focused opposition? Given the political might of entrenched special interests, what can be done to ensure that the common good prevails? Certainly a cookie-cutter approach will not do. In addressing infrastructure vulnerabilities to terrorist threats, natural disasters, and aging, America needs to recognize there are several models available. For maximum results, the nation should pursue a three-step process. Governments should address the need for the protection and maintenance of infrastructure and facilities by using a risk-based approach. That is the starting point. Not just the federal government, but state and local governments also need to use the model designed to counter terrorist threats in their efforts to identify the critical infrastructure that is most vulnerable.

Second, federal agencies, from the Department of Transportation to the Departments of Energy and Treasury, should examine the top 500 to 1,000 high-consequence and high-risk assets in their efforts to begin planning on how best to reduce vulnerabilities. If each state assessed its own infrastructure, the nation as a whole would have a better picture of the protection and maintenance required to ensure continued functioning during natural disasters and emergencies.

Once the most vulnerable assets are identified, a strategy for maintenance and protection can proceed. This strategy needs to estimate the cost of long-term maintenance on the existing infrastructure, and also whether further building should be limited in naturally vulnerable areas where the cost of protection to society far outweighs the benefit to a small number of individuals such as developers. After this strategy is developed, it has to be funded, implemented, and continued for years to come. I have witnessed how worthy projects begin with a great deal of hoopla and public support, only to watch commitment wane once the television lights are off and the media move on to the next issue. The plan to protect America's infrastructure and facilities cannot be executed in a week, month, or year. By definition, it is long-term in nature. It will require a sustained commitment and follow-through, year after year, for generations to come. This approach is necessary if Americans want to protect their nation and their fellow citizens.

The bottom line is that America's critical infrastructure will be in place well beyond the term of today's elected officials. It will outlast the normal politicking and funding conflicts that arise with every budget cycle. Now is the time to mount a long-term, comprehensive national strategy designed to preserve that infrastructure. We can build on the strategy already in place that guards against terrorist threats and apply that same disciplined approach to the challenges generated by nature and the passage of time. Now is the time for an active strategy based on all that America has learned from the past. By necessity this approach should be a partnership, but when necessary it may require strong government action to minimize risk. This strategy should reflect a partnership committed to applying every tool available to the matter at hand. In the end, planning is everything. The Gulf Coast evacuation during Hurricane Gustav succeeded because we had spent three years planning, building, and working to improve the system. Given a long-term focus on protecting and maintaining infrastructure, the nation will be able to rest in the knowledge that when the next catastrophe strikes, governments and industries had done all they could to protect life and property. We will have provided a service not just for this generation, but for those to come.

# Cybersecurity

O F the many challenges facing the global economy in the twenty-first century, one of the most complex and potentially consequential is the threat of a large-scale cyber attack against shared information technology and cyber infrastructure, including the Internet. The exponential growth of the Internet over the past two decades has created manifold benefits for society and the economy, but with these benefits has come a commensurate increase in cyber threats and vulnerabilities, making it imperative to act with urgency and purpose to protect the cyber domain from crippling attacks and disruptions.

Of course, the world of cyberspace is one in which we are unlikely to see airplanes crashing into buildings or bombs exploding on trains. But we could see human and economic consequences that are very much on par with traditional acts of terrorism. A successful cyber attack could shut down essential government services, imperil business operations, erode public trust in financial transactions, and disrupt electronic communications. The impact of a cyber attack could be far-reaching indeed, threatening multiple sectors of the economy at once and creating cascading effects across interdependent systems and operations.

But while the potential consequences of a cyber attack are every bit as concerning as those of a physical attack, managing the risk is not the same. Cybersecurity is not exclusively or even largely a government responsibility or something that can be imposed on businesses or individual users of the Internet. In the United States, the federal government does not own the information technology networks or communications infrastructure, and it would not want to force a burdensome and intrusive security regime on one of the most dynamic and reliable engines of the U.S. economy.

Yet cybersecurity is not solely a private sector responsibility either. The private sector may own the vast majority of cyber infrastructure, but its benefits are so widely distributed across the public domain and so integrated into various sectors of the economy—from banking and energy to transportation and communications—that everyone faces clear security risks and consequences if the infrastructure is not adequately protected.

Further complicating matters, we know that no single person or entity controls the Internet or IT infrastructure and that there is no centralized node, database, or entry point. No single person, company, or government can fully protect the IT infrastructure. And a security failure in even one company, or at just one link of the chain, can have a cascading effect on everybody else.

How do we address this shared problem in an era of increasing global dependency on cyber systems and infrastructure? How do we ensure the integrity of the Internet without compromising its fundamental openness and fluidity and unique culture? And how do we minimize the impact of cyber attacks while increasing economic and communications resiliency?

## Recognizing Cyber Threats

It is important to understand the serious nature of the current threat. The Internet has been around for roughly two decades. For about the same amount of time, we have also seen cyber attacks in one form or another. Some may be tempted to suggest that cyber attacks are merely a cost of doing business—a nuisance dealt with in the past that can be readily dealt with in the future—and that there is no real reason to treat this threat as a concerted national or international priority. I think this would be a misguided approach.

The U.S. intelligence community has publicly stated its assessment that some nations, including Russia and China, have the technical capability to target and disrupt parts of the information infrastructure, or to use that infrastructure to collect intelligence and other kinds of information. Nation-states and criminal groups target governmental and private sector information networks to gain competitive advantage in the commercial sector, as well as in the area of security.

Terrorist groups, including Al Qaeda, Hamas, and Hezbollah, have expressed the desire to launch attacks on cyber infrastructure. Criminal elements show a growing and alarming sophistication in technical capability and targeting, operating a pervasive, mature economy in illicit cyber capabilities and services that are available to anybody willing to pay.

Cyber threats can impact individuals and nations alike. During the Georgia-Russia conflict in 2008, we saw perhaps the first instance of military action with a clear cyber component. The denial of service attacks launched from Russian IP addresses against Georgia occurred with military action against the Georgian government. A large number of Georgians could not access any information about what was happening in their country. Government websites were defaced and the delivery of government information and services was curtailed.

In the United States, criminal networks have exploited cyber systems for significant personal gain. In August 2008, the federal government disrupted the largest cyber identity theft ring in U.S. history, involving 40 million credit card numbers stolen from nine major retailers through a sophisticated, international scheme perpetrated by capturing wireless transmissions of information from commercial computer systems. This scheme led to the withdrawal of millions of dollars from the bank accounts of innocent consumers across the world.

The reality is that cyber attacks are not decreasing; in fact, they are increasing in frequency, sophistication, and scope. They include a broad range of nefarious activity: a single individual or an organized criminal group trying to steal personal or financial information; a hacker trying to breach a system to show that he or she can do it; nation states engaged in cyber espionage against governments and businesses. There is also the prospect of a terrorist group hijacking and exploiting the Internet to cause very real damage to information and communications systems and to the economy.

## Defending Systems and Networks

All these threats have major implications for national and economic security. As such, they raise the question of how best to address them.

The first thing we must do is ensure that government networks are adequately protected. In essence, we need to look across government's civilian domains to assess vulnerabilities, reduce points of access to the Internet that could be sources of intrusion, put into effect tools that will reduce or eliminate the possibility of an attack, and use around-the-clock monitoring to stay ahead of an evolving adversary.

In January 2008, President Bush issued a classified national and homeland security directive that for the first time will unify, accelerate, and expand the U.S. government's cybersecurity efforts under a Comprehensive National Cybersecurity Initiative. This "Cyber Initiative" has three major components: establishing clear lines of defense, defending against all threats, and shaping the future environment by educating the next generation of cyber professionals as well as producing new, game-changing technologies.

As part of this effort, the U.S. government will continue to ensure that privacy and civil liberties considerations are at the center of cybersecurity. The government has no interest in sitting over the Internet or attempting to control what people see. No government should disrupt the open architecture and culture of freedom that are the hallmarks of the Internet—to do so would undermine the very thing we must try to protect.

In the United States, the federal government currently faces a situation in which it has thousands of connection points between government domains, civilian domains, and the Internet. This is simply too many and creates unnecessary vulnerabilities. To build a set of capable defenses, the number of connections must be limited. The government is now in the process of reducing the number of connections to fewer than one hundred.

In addition to reducing potential avenues of attack, government must have robust monitoring of and proper coordination between agencies. Every part of the civilian network must have appropriate levels of security for what is allowed to enter from the Internet and must show how system security will be maintained. A single weak link could compromise the entire system. To provide this coordination, the Department of Homeland Security has established a new National Cyber Security Center to improve overall threat awareness and to ensure coordination among various federal cyber centers.

DHS has also taken action to expand and strengthen its intrusion detection system, known as "Einstein." This system sounds the alert if a malicious intrusion has occurred, providing information about the signature and code of the attack, which we can disseminate to agencies across the network. We are in the process of deploying a more advanced system that will enable us to detect, in real time, if an attack is under way. In the future, the department intends to move from intrusion detection to intrusion prevention, ultimately developing a system that will allow us to actually stop an attack before it permeates and infects our systems.

The second focus of the U.S. Cyber Initiative is to protect against a full complement of threats: not only threats from hackers, criminals, nation states, and terrorists, but also insider threats, such as individuals downloading sensitive information, including passwords, that will afford them access to a system, or planting a bug that would enable the capture of information over the Internet. Although this is a relatively unsophisticated threat, it can cause as much damage as a traditional cyber attack.

Protection must also be provided against compromised hardware or software that has been embedded in electronic devices during manufacture or before they are sold on the open market. This is a particularly difficult challenge in a global environment where the components of a finished product are often produced in multiple places or countries, each with uneven quality control.

To counter these types of threats, steps must be taken to protect the global supply chain, and we must work with the private sector to achieve better validation of the source of critical elements of software and hardware, particularly for systems that contain high value, sensitive information. At the same time, governments must continue to use old-fashioned counter-intelligence: working to prevent people from committing espionage, stealing data or passwords, or implanting trapdoors in systems.

The third and final element of the Cyber Initiative is to shape the future environment by recruiting and developing the next generation of cybersecurity professionals. Specifically, it involves working with the private sector to boost cyber education, training, and recruitment, as well as funding for leap-ahead technology and game-changing capabilities that will increase cybersecurity at an accelerated pace. Just as past generations of highly skilled workers met the challenges of their times, we must build a new generation of cyber professionals to address the current threat.

## Expanding Partnerships

Ultimately, the value of the Internet and the vast social and commercial activity it enables will only continue to multiply if its users are confident they will not lose their identities or their sensitive information when they enter cyberspace. The government alone cannot provide such assurance, nor can it mandate a top-down, command-and-control approach to a fundamentally decentralized, networked system.

On the contrary—securing cyberspace will require an unprecedented series of partnerships among the public and private sectors, owners and operators of cyber infrastructure, businesses, and even individual users. To build such partnerships, the federal government has reached across all sectors to set goals and priorities and exchange information about security as it relates to a particular sector's threats and vulnerabilities. DHS has asked the private sector to look at cyber risks and mitigations as well as interdependencies that could affect multiple sectors and have cascading consequences on their ability to function. We also have explored the possibility of sharing federal capabilities, including our intrusion detection system, so the private sector can benefit from our efforts on a voluntary basis if it chooses.

Because managing risk is often an inexact science, DHS is working with the private sector to establish metrics that will allow us to chart our progress and focus on how to mitigate risks apparent in the globalization of the commercial technology industry. It is important to create standards that will allow the private sector to gauge the integrity of the systems it purchases: it must have confidence in what it is getting on the open market and what it is delivering to its customers. Recently, we have seen a rising concern in the global environment about the safety of and potential contaminants in certain foods and toys. The security of software and hardware that finds its way into homes and businesses must also be of great concern.

Finally, individual citizens have an important role to play in cybersecurity. Simple steps taken at home or work can have an immense impact on overall protection and will help increase defenses. For example, individuals can ensure that antivirus software is properly functioning and up-to-date, change passwords regularly and keep from writing them down, and avoid suspicious emails and websites. Unfortunately, too many individuals fail to take these steps on a regular basis, creating unnecessary vulnerability.

## The Challenges Ahead

The challenge of cybersecurity is both significant and complex. Achieving effective regulatory governance in this area calls for a comprehensive strategy that involves coordinated action by government, the private sector, and individual citizens. Of course, an undertaking of this size and magnitude cannot be completed overnight—it requires a sustained, multiyear effort with significant governmental and private sector cooperation. More than anything, it will require developing and sustaining a sense of urgency and commitment because unfortunately the threat is mounting. The global community has a clear, common interest in protecting the security of cyber systems which calls for immediate action and cooperation, as well as ongoing attention and study.

# Responding to IEDs at Home

I N the post-9/11 world, securing the homeland involves the un-
pleasant task of thinking the way the terrorists do. This entails
surveying all the possible ways in which they can attack the United
States again, and then deciding how best to defend against these
various scenarios. And as we continue to plan accordingly, we face
the further challenge of doing so in a way that respects our culture,
commerce, and way of life.

Although the nation can and must protect against the possibility
of a terrorist strike through such weapons as biological infections or
chemical sprays, the vast majority of attacks worldwide continue to
be conducted with bombs. Typically, these are improvised explosive
devices (IEDs), as opposed to manufactured explosives used by a
conventional military force. IEDs have been deployed extensively
by insurgents against coalition forces in Iraq, as well as by terrorists
throughout the world in recent years. And lest we forget, within
our own borders, the Oklahoma City bombing in 1995 was an IED

attack. Unquestionably, any strategy against terrorism must be one that counters the threat posed by improvised explosive devices.

There are four main facets of our strategy of countering these devices. First, we recognize the critical importance of intelligence. Obviously, adequate and accurate intelligence can help prevent attacks. Moreover, the more precise the information we have about the source of a threat, the easier it is to narrow our security focus. The result is reduced disruption of daily life and inconvenience to most people, and a much more efficient use of our resources to prevent bad things from happening.

Absent sufficient information and intelligence, we are compelled to cast a wider security net. We are forced to consider broader countermeasures such as inspecting the contents of passenger bags on mass transit systems, which would result in more inconvenience and disruption. Those who on privacy grounds seek to restrict our ability to obtain intelligence fail to take this into account.

A second facet of DHS strategy against IEDs involves forging and strengthening the bonds of partnerships. It begins with the recognition that this is not just a federal problem, but one that concerns state and local governments and ultimately the private sector as well. Clearly, the business community has a role to play, not just in building the architecture of protection but on issues relating to the control of materials that could be used to make bombs.

A third strategy aspect is a reliance on people to be vigilant and to report any anomalous or suspicious activity to the authorities. In 2007, for example, the disruption of the plot to set off bombs in London and Glasgow began with an ambulance driver in London, who notified the police about the way a car was parked outside a nightclub. And in 2001, Richard Reid was prevented from lighting his shoe bomb on an airplane by alert citizens.

And finally, the threat posed by IEDs must be viewed in a multilayered, full-spectrum fashion. From the coalescing of dangerous individuals into a group to their hatching a plot to attack, from their assembling an IED to their detonating it at a critical site, we see opportunities along the continuum to thwart them from achieving their goals.

Certainly, we seek the earliest possible intervention. Ideally, we want to go directly after the terrorists and their organizations before their plots can be executed. We can do this through intercepting their communications, interfering with their receipt of funds, and keeping them away from our country or dangerous materials out of their hands. Doing all of this effectively constitutes the best possible outcome; it is the execution of a successful prevention strategy.

Besides prevention, the next best outcome is successful detection and disruption of actual plots against the United States. Failing that, we rely on protection—an on-site presence to block a bomb from being detonated. If in spite of these efforts an IED is detonated, we want a preparedness and response system that can spring quickly into action and minimize the impact on people and infrastructure, denying the terrorists the full measure of victory they seek. And finally, along with this response, we seek successful attribution, the ability to work backward and find the culprits responsible for the attack.

## Responding to the IED Threat

Prevention, detection, protection, and response—these cover the spectrum or continuum of how DHS is handling the IED threat to the nation.

Concerning prevention, if we are unable to expel or incapacitate a dangerous individual who wants to detonate an IED in our country, we can at least make it harder for him to obtain the materials needed to produce it. For years, the large concentration of chemicals located at plants or transit facilities near heavily populated areas presented a tempting opportunity that such individuals could potentially exploit. In 2007, at our urging, Congress passed new chemical security laws permitting us to issue the kinds of regulations needed to confront this high-consequence risk. Specifically, it enabled us to require certain chemical facilities to identify vulnerabilities to their locations and to develop and implement site security plans that include measures that satisfy risk-based security standards.

An even higher-consequence risk is that terrorists and other dangerous people could produce IEDs enhanced with radioactive material. A "dirty bomb" would be considerably worse than a conventional bomb of the same size, partly because it would contaminate affected areas, and partly because of the psychological effect it would have on the country and its people. Unfortunately, the material for a dirty bomb is not hard to obtain or to add to an IED.

In response to this threat, the country needs to further strengthen the controls on powerful materials like cesium 137. While these are important radiological materials used in a variety of medical and other legitimate functions, the fact that they can be added to IEDs to produce particularly lethal dirty bombs cannot be ignored. What is needed is a risk management approach, not the banning of these otherwise useful substances, but stronger measures in conjunction with the Nuclear Regulatory Commission that balance our need for these substances with the imperative to keep them out of lethal hands.

Besides keeping such materials away from terrorists and other dangerous people, another preventive step against the detonation of IEDs involves the sharing of information and best practices with our state, local, and private sector partners. To that end, our Office of Bombing Prevention developed and launched the TRIPwire secure information sharing portal. Essentially, TRIPwire collects what we have learned about IEDs and makes it available to state and local agencies as well as to other federal departments and the business community. Through our grant programs, we are helping state and local governments turn the information we provide into the necessary tools to prevent, detect, and, if necessary, disarm bombs. We have assisted state and local jurisdictions in creating underwater terrorism prevention plans for 60 high-risk ports across the nation, enhancing their ability to do such things as detect and detonate bombs.

Clearly, there is much we are doing and can do in the future in the preventive arena against the threat of an IED strike. But it would be folly to rely on prevention alone, on our ability to disrupt each and every plot hatched against the homeland. Assuming we fail to disrupt a particular plot and are protecting a specific location from an attack, our next step would be to detect the device before it exploded.

When it comes to detection strategies, location matters. If the location is Iraq, the U.S. military faces more potential IED attackers than we do at home. But, on the other hand, Iraq has no vast, open transportation infrastructure like a subway system to protect. Moreover, from a risk management perspective, putting the kinds of detection measures we have in Iraq in U.S. subway systems would likely destroy the ability of the systems to function.

Unquestionably, detection capabilities must be configured to the reality of the architecture in which we operate. A good example is at our airports, where the Transportation Security Administration has deployed more than 1,500 explosive detection and 7,400 explosive trace detection systems around the country to screen carry-on baggage.

DHS has succeeded in building multiple layers of defenses at our airports. Among them is the Bomb Appraisal Officer Program, which supports screeners with additional technical capability, allowing them to identify more difficult-to-detect types of bomb components and detonators. Besides seeking to detect dangerous items like bombs, some airport personnel are also being trained to detect potentially dangerous individuals through a technique known as behavioral observation. This technique has been borrowed from the Israelis and from European security officers who are trained to pick out individuals from among the crowds whose behavior might suggest nefarious aims. Fortunately, behavioral observation techniques are far more predictive of individual intent than the long-discredited tactic of racial or ethnic profiling which relies on appearance or national origin.

Randomness is a second critical tool in helping detect dangerous individuals or items threatening the country and key infrastructure. Since terrorists are inveterate planners, we can thwart their ability to execute their plans by introducing an element of randomness in our detection techniques. We deploy hundreds of detection canine teams on a random basis. Combining select members of the Coast Guard, Transportation Security Administration, and other law enforcement groups, we have formed Visual Intermodal Prevention and Response teams that can move suddenly into airports.

DHS will, of course, continue to work to develop game-changing tools that enhance our capabilities to detect explosives. These will include detection equipment using new technology that can transcend the current limitations of the trace technology and the other detection devices we currently have. They will entail increased study of behavioral analysis and subliminal cues that can be picked up either mechanically or through the training of officers.

But just as we cannot guarantee that our preventive measures will thwart every plot, we also cannot ensure that our detection techniques will identify every dangerous person carrying a lethal item like an IED. That is why we need to identify vulnerable assets and protect or harden them. How do we harden them? We have developed more than 2,000 buffer-zone protection plans to strengthen high-risk sites and communities against the possibility of a direct attack from an individual or a vehicle-borne explosive device.

Mindful of attacks like that against the USS *Cole* in 2000, we have worked hard to strengthen the security of our ports, focusing especially on explosive devices planted in cargo containers. In line with this concern is our determination to engage in more robust screening and inspection of small boats. It is interesting how some of the most vocal advocates of increased container security have failed to raise their voices on the need for protecting our ports against the threat of small vessels loaded with IEDs and other explosives.

In addition to dealing with the issue of small boats, we are also confronting security issues relating to general aviation arriving from overseas. We are doing more under new regulations to require information about who or what is coming in on those private jets.

## Response Capabilities

I have cited how we aim to stop a successful IED attack through prevention, detection, and protection strategies. But what if these strategies fail? Then we must rely on our response capabilities. Even as we work hard to prevent an attack, we must also plan and prepare for the worst, so that if and when it does occur, we can respond in a way that minimizes the consequences and saves the maximum number of lives.

To ensure the kind of effective response we need, there is simply no substitute for rigorous planning, preparing, and training. To this end, top officials from every level of government, as well as representatives from the private sector and international community, regularly engage in the nation's premier terrorism preparedness exercise. Known as TOPOFF, this exercise addresses key issues of prevention and response and tests the ability of participants to make tough decisions and carry out essential functions in the aftermath of a simulated incident of national significance.

On 15–19 October 2007, the TOPOFF exercise included responding to a hypothetical IED attack. As part of that response, firefighters in Portland, Oregon, were able to enter the affected area using radiological detection devices. These were the devices they routinely wear when moving into an area where there has been an explosion. This exercise enabled us to get a swift heads-up that under the scenario it wasn't just a conventional but a radiological device. And that has enormous consequences in terms of informing people what to do, and ultimately in mitigating the damage.

Since September 11, the United States has been spared the kinds of bombing attacks that have been launched in countries across much of the globe. This should lead us neither to complacency over being spared, nor to hysteria over the fact that we live in a dangerous and unpredictable world. Rather, it should lead to a determined resolve to continue our risk-based approach against IEDs and other threats. It is an approach and a strategy that has served us well, strengthening our security while preserving our liberty.

# 10

# Managing Identity

With the pervasive use of the Internet for business transactions, the issue of identity increasingly lies at the heart of the global financial and economic system. If sellers, for example, cannot rely on the information they are receiving about the identity of buyers, this can seriously inhibit global economic progress and growth.

For the United States and other countries, the problem of identity fraud presents an especially urgent homeland security problem. A number of nations, including the United States, face the daily threat of people attempting to enter and work illegally—as well as the prospect of terrorists, and other dangerous individuals, entering countries and ultimately achieving their deadly aims—by pretending to be who they are not.

Indeed, in the United States, the 9/11 Commission expended considerable effort addressing the question of vulnerability and weakness in our identity systems prior to the September 11 attacks from the perspective of national security. It analyzed the risk of dangerous people using fraudulent identification to cross our borders, pass through our airports and seaports, board planes, or walk into federal government buildings.

When such individuals specifically masquerade as other people by stealing their identity, this becomes not just a national security challenge, but also a personal security problem. And as countless identity theft victims can attest, it can quickly become a financial security problem and a reputational one as well.

A 2008 story in the *Wall Street Journal* provides a grim example of how identity crimes affect ordinary people.[1] It related the harrowing ordeal of a woman from California who found herself a hapless victim of such illegal activity. The trouble started in 2003, when she received a letter from the Internal Revenue Service (IRS) concerning $18,000 in unreported income. In fact, she never worked for the company in question, which was located 3,000 miles away in North Carolina. Nonetheless, she continued to receive letters from the IRS, and eventually calls from collection agencies for medical, furniture, and cell phone charges. As her husband told the reporter of the story, "My wife would jump up every time the phone would ring. In the middle of the night, she would wake up afraid and just sit in bed."

It turned out that an illegal worker at the North Carolina company had stolen her name and Social Security number in order to get hired and proceeded to use these identity markers for her own purposes. It took five long and difficult years for the woman to clear her name with the IRS and creditors.

This disturbing story underscores how the matter of identity touches nearly every element of a country's social fabric. In the arena of employment alone, it relates to several concerns: how an employer ascertains whether workers are who they say they are so their backgrounds can be checked, whether they are entitled to work so firms know they are complying with the law, and whether they are connected to the name in various tax databases so employers can be certain that when they withhold payroll taxes, the money is actually going to the right person, not an imposter.

As seen in the experience of the California victim, the significant human costs of identity theft should be plainly evident to all. What is far less visible are the financial costs to society, which tend to be greatly understated and obscured from public view. That is because businesses such as credit card companies quietly absorb fraud-related charges, deeming them "acceptable losses." Cardholders do not necessarily know when such losses occur. Often they will not be notified about the fact that their credit-card company has success-fully thwarted an effort to use their name in order to falsely acquire goods. Some firms fail to report identity-related losses to the government because of concerns about liability and reputation.

I can attest to the magnitude of the global identity challenge. On 5 August 2008 I announced what may be the largest prosecution of identity theft in United States history. With the unsealing of indictments in Boston and San Diego, 11 individuals from around the world were charged with participating in the theft and sale of more than 40 million credit and debit card numbers from eight major U.S. retailers.

Clearly, by any measure, the world faces an identity management challenge of escalating proportions. This is certainly a twenty-first-century problem, but unfortunately, the world has yet to begin implementing twenty-first-century solutions.

## A New Era for Identity Protection

In the United States and throughout much of the world, governments have long relied on two key means of identity protection. The first is the use of cards or documents, such as passports or driver's licenses. The second involves the use of a password or identification number, such as a Social Security number, which authenticates users, enabling them to be eligible for a job, engage in a transaction, or access a bank account.

Unfortunately, cards or documents can be forged or counterfeited, and numbers lost or misused. Several of the September 11 hijackers obtained drivers' licenses illegally and the experience of the California identity theft victim highlights the ability of law-breakers to obtain and misuse the Social Security numbers of innocent, unsuspecting individuals.

When it comes to words and numbers as identity protectors, society is faced with a vexing paradox: The more these identity protectors are relied upon, the more pervasive they become. And with ubiquity comes a dramatically higher cost of losing control of them. Using a number or word to authenticate identity puts control of identity into the hands of those doing the authenticating. Even if all these people are honest, they now have access to key confidential identity information; the more people who have this information, the more likely it will be lost and eventually misused by others.

What can we do about this?

With respect to cards or documents, we are making it harder to counterfeit or forge them. We are installing chips in passports, creating secure Pass Cards using bar codes, and embedding forms of holograms in our identification documents.

Both the 9/11 Commission and Congress recognized that the status quo at U.S. borders, where more than 8,000 kinds of documents—including foreign baptismal certificates and even library cards—were accepted as proof of identity, was unacceptable and unworkable and had to be changed. In response to this need, we are implementing the Western Hemisphere Travel Initiative (WHTI). Through WHTI, we are taking the necessary steps to insist on secure travel documentation for people within the hemisphere who are crossing U.S. land, sea, and air borders. We are also implementing the Transport Worker

Identification Credential (TWIC) initiative, which provides secure identification cards for port workers.

The United States has also come to realize that driver's licenses and other state-issued identification documents must be made more secure. Consequently, through our REAL ID initiative, we are strengthening the security of state driver's licenses by establishing uniform standards for states to follow as they create and issue them. We are also safeguarding numerical authenticators such as Social Security and PIN numbers through encryption.

## Privacy Concerns

These efforts can and will reduce identity vulnerabilities in the United States, as well as in other countries that pursue similar strategies. Nonetheless, as it institutes these measures, the U.S. government is confronted with two sets of persistent challenges—arguments about privacy and questions about long-term efficacy. Regarding privacy, there are three arguments that often appear in discussions of identity management.

The first argument essentially asserts an unconditional right to anonymity. Advocates argue that it is simply wrong to demand identification of any kind. I agree that there should be a right to anonymity regarding most human actions such as walking down a street. While a number of European nations require an identification card at all times, a reasonable case can be made that in an open forum, such as a block or street, individuals normally should be able to move along without having to produce proof of identity.

But should the right to anonymity be absolute? Do all individuals have a fundamental, unabridged right never to provide proof of who they are? Do they have the right to cross any border without having to furnish evidence of who they are? Certainly, any nation is justified in wanting to know who is seeking entry, so it can decide whether or not to admit that person. This is analogous to a family, which has the right to determine who can enter the family home and to require proof of identity for strangers who are claiming special reasons for admission, such as conducting health inspections.

The same holds true of boarding a passenger plane. Few would argue against requiring identification for every passenger. Given the obvious risk of a terrorist boarding and then converting the plane into a weapon or blowing it up, most people would agree that the right to anonymity must yield to the right of other passengers on the plane to self-preservation. Here is a thought experiment. Imagine an airline that would allow total anonymity for its passengers. Would that airline have passengers or even pilots? I suspect not. Few would be willing to assume the dramatically increased risk resulting from a misguided policy of anonymity for passengers.

In fact, those who argue for total anonymity often forget that in any situation where a person is asked for identification, there is another person or entity involved—the one who is doing the asking. Both parties have rights. A person has the right to choose whether to disclose his or her identity. But the person with whom one is dealing has the right to know with whom he or she is doing business, and to refrain from doing so with those who decline disclosure. To assert an absolute right to anonymity is to deprive another of the right to decline a transaction.

This system is driven by the same basic principles as the caller ID model of identification. When caller ID was first distributed widely, opponents protested that this forced callers to have their phone numbers revealed to recipients. The solution? Allow callers to hide their phone numbers by pressing a button or two. In this way, callers retain a right to anonymity. In turn, recipients can see when callers are withholding identity and refuse to speak to them.

In other words, when it comes to boarding planes and other transactional activities, the problem with total anonymity is that it only protects one set of rights. In contrast, the caller ID model honors both privacy rights and security concerns. The logic is clear. One can ask for identification. The person who is asked can refuse to provide it and remain anonymous. In response to this refusal, the identifier can refrain from dealing with the unidentified person.

The claim of an unconditional right to anonymity constitutes one kind of privacy argument or objection. A second kind concedes that identification must sometimes be required, but refuses to let government set standards for the identity documents. This is a fundamentally illogical objection. What good is allowing proof of identity if we disallow efforts to secure it from being falsified or stolen? Are we truly prepared to argue for an inalienable right of people to lie about who they are and to steal other people's identities or create fictitious identities for themselves? For all intents and purposes, this is an argument for insecure identification, which is of course a contradiction in terms.

In addition to these two privacy objections, there is, however, a third, more practical privacy argument. It is that some of the tools we use to protect identity are not effective or may actually create new vulnerabilities. And that requires a discussion of the second challenge the United States faces in its efforts to enhance identity management—the question of ultimate efficacy.

Surely it is wise to respond to our identity vulnerabilities by seeking to make the current system better. Clearly it is prudent to pursue ways of making identity documents more difficult to forge or counterfeit. Of course it makes sense to utilize encryption to safeguard various forms of numerical authentication. While these efforts are necessary, they are insufficient in dealing with the identity problem in its entirety. Simply stated, they are twentieth-century fixes to a twentieth-century system facing a twenty-first-century challenge. And to the extent that they are insufficient, they fail to deal fully with identity theft both as a security problem *and* a privacy violation. What is needed is a broader, more comprehensive approach. There is such an approach available, one that can be neatly summed up in three words: description, device, and digit.

## The Three Ds

An identity description refers to a piece of information or something known to an individual and to that person alone, something which separates that individual from all others, including identity thieves. In the United States, Social Security numbers, mother's birth name, or passwords are common examples. An identity device refers an identity card or document of some sort. It could also be a cell phone or computer to be used for identification. Some computerized devices require insertion of a token that changes every 30 seconds, so that the number flashing on the token becomes useless if stolen, because after 30 seconds have passed, it no longer grants access. There are many individuals who currently use their cell phones as ID devices. They access the Internet with their Blackberry® or conduct business using their Blackberry® over the Internet.

As mentioned, our standard twentieth-century identity security practices have long used ID descriptions in the form of words or numbers, and ID devices in the form of cards or documents.

In order to create a truly twenty-first-century system, we now need to combine descriptions and devices with the third element mentioned above: a digit. An identity digit, also known as a biometric, refers to one's finger. One's digits or fingers are unique, as evidenced by one's fingerprints. Given their uniqueness, they make ideal identifiers or ways that we can separate real people from impersonators. Simply stated, fingerprints do not lie. Applied alone, identity descriptions and devices are inadequate guarantors of identity protection. But when combined with each other and with digits, a far more effective security system emerges. The way forward is to work with all three of these tools in concert. One day, we will be able to combine all "3-Ds": a personal identification number (description) with an identity card or cell phone (device) and a "digit" (fingerprints). Once we do, we will have taken a quantum leap forward on behalf of secure identity. Such an identity combination could be used for authentication in virtually any setting that calls for it, from boarding a plane to transacting business at a bank to entering a student dormitory.

Would this be a perfect solution to the identity dilemma? Perhaps. There will undoubtedly be exceptionally cunning and determined individuals who will find a way to steal someone's device, obtain and fabricate fingerprints, and then steal the PIN number. But the odds of all three events occurring are very low indeed. And while the "3-D" solution would not produce perfect identity security, it would improve it dramatically. Taken together, these are some of the key steps needed to bring identity management into the twenty-first century.

The identity management challenge appears daunting, but as we look over the horizon, we see the outlines of a set of solutions that will make the United States and people around the world freer, safer, and more secure. We should do what we can to hasten its arrival, for the benefit of people everywhere.

# PREPARATION
# AND RESPONSE

# Managing Risk

W HAT is the greatest risk that nations face today? Some would say it is the danger posed by global terrorism. Others would point to the prospect of continued financial or economic turmoil. Still others would stress natural disasters like earthquakes, tsunamis, or hurricanes.

In fact, the principal risk we face is that we will fail to address adequately these and other serious threats to life, safety, and security. The world, including the United States, must manage risk properly: in a sustained, forward-looking fashion that seeks to mitigate risk without vainly attempting to eliminate it. In the United States, it is clear from the 9/11 terrorist attacks, from the uneven preparations for natural disasters like hurricanes, and from the current financial crisis that our society has inadequately applied sound risk management principles to its challenges.

To confront these challenges, the United States, as well as the rest of the world, must correct the systemic shortcomings of the current risk management paradigm. In three key areas—misaligned time horizons, negative externalities, and transaction costs arising from lack of transparency—governments must regulate markets in ways that effectively manage the shared consequences of individual decisions.

## The Costs of Inadequate Risk Management

In the aftermath of September 11, the 9/11 Commission painstakingly catalogued the ways in which the United States had neglected to prepare for a large-scale terrorist attack and take the necessary steps to reduce the chances of such an event happening. As the Commission noted, the general warning signs of some kind of attack were evident for years. The World Trade Center had been struck by terrorists in 1993, eight years before its destruction on 9/11. In 1998, three years prior to the September 11 atrocities, Osama bin Laden had declared war against the United States and urged his minions to target American civilians as well as the U.S. military. That same year, terrorists devastated two American embassy locations in Africa, and, in 2000, they bombed the U.S.S. *Cole*. Meanwhile, report after report unavailingly stressed the need to strengthen our homeland security. Clearly, the nation misjudged the risk of a high-consequence terrorist attack on its soil.

With respect to hurricanes like Katrina, which devastated New Orleans and its environs in 2005, Americans have known for decades that such storms exist and that they often make landfall in coastal states like Louisiana, Mississippi, and Texas. Likewise, Americans have long known that it is a recipe for disaster to allow unregulated growth and development while failing to maintain protective infrastructure, especially in areas below sea level. Yet prior to Hurricane Katrina's arrival, government at all levels did not restrain risky housing development or invest in maintaining New Orleans's levees and canals. Katrina was a serious storm, but it was the breach of the ill-maintained levees that made it the costliest natural disaster in America's history.

And finally, the current financial crisis was predicted as far back as the 1990s, when economists began to warn of the consequences of housing and financial bubbles driven by excessive leverage and credit, and of a system characterized by mounting indebtedness.

In each of these instances, after the disaster struck, both the public and private sector took action by investing enormous time, effort, and resources in response. Responding to disasters after they occur is not risk management; it is compensating for the adverse consequences of risk *mis*management. Managing risk is not about looking back at disasters that already have happened. Rather, it is looking ahead to disasters that have yet to happen, with the goal of preventing or reducing our vulnerabilities or mitigating the consequences if disasters do in fact occur. Proper risk assessment and risk-mitigating action *before* the event tends to be far less costly and could prevent the crisis from arising in the first place.

Worse yet is when society fails to learn lessons from previous disasters fueled by unmanaged risks. The result is the emergence of a disturbing cycle. After disaster strikes, money is poured into risk reduction in order to prevent its recurrence. But as time passes and the vivid imagery of the disaster fades from public consciousness, society begins to retreat from its commitment to risk reduction, making future disasters more likely. In the wake of September 11, the United States moved decisively and effectively to create a new Department of Homeland Security, remove some of the barriers between intelligence agencies, hunt for Al Qaeda leaders overseas, and institute numerous measures to prevent or reduce our vulnerability to further attacks. Now, ironically, because no successful attack has been launched against the United States in intervening years, a growing chorus is proclaiming the threat to have passed and is urging us to relax our risk management posture.

After Katrina, when those who failed or were unable to evacuate found themselves trapped in their homes, the vow was that this must not happen again. Yet just three years after Katrina, when Hurricane Gustav was barreling toward New Orleans, some residents decided they would rather ride out the storm than leave. Fortunately, Gustav was considerably less catastrophic than feared and the vast majority of people were evacuated through effective work at all levels of government. However, it remains unclear whether enough individuals will heed a future evacuation order when the next potentially serious hurricane approaches their shore.

In short, it is imperative that the issue of risk be handled intelligently and consistently, with a critical eye toward the future. But who owns the responsibility for managing risk? Government? Business? Individuals? In free societies, the starting point for addressing risk management is the delineation of the roles that should be played by individuals and businesses and those that should be played by government.

## Toward Principled Risk Management

Individuals and businesses routinely balance risk and reward, as well as costs and benefits, on their own. Clearly, their self-interest lies in doing this well. Since they know the details of their own situation best, they tend to do a better job of making risk-focused and cost-benefit calculations for their own lives. Free-market principles reflect our preference for making these individual choices.

Letting the free-market process run its natural course usually works well. But it would be a mistake to claim that government has no role to play in the free market or that the free market can really be unbounded or unregulated. Implicit in the freedom of the marketplace are government rules that enable the market to function, such as the enforcement of contracts or the enforcement of criminal laws that bar people from robbing one another. Remove these rules, and free markets will disintegrate.

Given that government does have an affirmative role to play in the free market, the question is not if, but when and how government intervention is appropriate to foster risk management in the marketplace and society as a whole. In my view, there are three classic types of cases in which government action is necessary and prudent in order to ensure proper risk management: the misaligned time horizon, externalized costs, and business transparency. In these areas, individual risk management seems to fail due to market imperfections; the government must shape rules to correct these failures.

The first failure, the misaligned time horizon, has to do with the mismatch between short-term benefits and long-term costs. In the real world, free markets and their participants favor the short term over the long term in deciding how much risk to bear. They often favor choices that produce short-term benefits over long-term benefits with potentially higher short-term costs. Particularly when these costs are uncertain, the result is a failure to manage against long-term risks.

This is what I call the "musical chairs" approach to risk management. Everybody realizes that a chair will be pulled away, leaving one person without a seat, but nobody knows when. Each person hopes that while they are still in the room, the music will keep playing, that once it stops they will have already left, and that when the chair gets pulled, somebody else will fall down.

An example of "musical chairs" in action concerns hurricanes. It is undeniable that in a hurricane-prone coastal region, physically elevating homes is critical to minimizing or mitigating the risk of damage. However, in the short run, the cost of elevating is high and the benefit may only be realized decades later when a hurricane hits in exactly the right spot and a storm surge flows into the area where one's home was elevated.

Thus, for a lot of people, the decision to elevate involves a trade-off between the immediate sacrifice of a high cost and the possible benefit that might only be realized, if ever, at some point in the future. Unfortunately, this creates a powerful incentive to forgo elevation. In the United States, this means that when government tries to require the elevation of homes, it is often met by vociferous opposition by everyone—from local elected officials to developers.

Political will is needed to enforce regulations such as building codes. The alternative is to tell homeowners that if they do not elevate their homes, they won't be insured against hurricanes. But experience teaches that if a hurricane damages their homes, they will pressure governments to provide them with aid packages, and governments will give way in the face of immediate suffering. That sends exactly the wrong message, namely that people don't need to buy insurance to cover long-term risk, because government will bail them out should disaster occur. Thus in order to ensure that long-term risk is factored into the equation, government must step in before the flood by enforcing regulations such as building codes. Government involvement before the fact is critical to making sure that long-term risk is factored into cost/benefit analyses, ensuring that societies deal with this imperfection in the market.

External costs are a second case in which governments in free societies must influence the cost/benefit equation in favor of risk mitigation. Left to themselves, most individuals and businesses balance costs and benefits by internalizing their own costs but not the costs they impose on others. For example, if we examine common law cases of centuries ago, we will see situations where a person was dumping waste into a river and polluting property miles downstream. From the polluter's perspective, costs and benefits were fully internalized. The person had the benefit of easy waste disposal, without disposal costs since the river carried the waste away. Meanwhile, downstream, the other property owner faced cleanup costs with no attendant benefits. Over the course of time, the law developed the concept of nuisance, which gave the downstream owner the right to force the upstream polluter to desist from further dumping, or to be compensated.

Cost externalities are even more important—and more complicated—in an economically interdependent world. Take, for example, the operation of critical businesses like gasoline stations during emergencies. In every hurricane I have seen, a chief cornerstone of recovery is reestablishing electrical power. This requires workers to repair power lines and perhaps clean power plants so they can resume operating. But to do so they need their cars to bring them there. A problem arises when gas stations, like other businesses in the area, lack power, meaning they cannot pump gas and drivers cannot refuel. This is exactly what happened in certain areas of the U.S. Gulf Coast during Hurricane Rita in 2005.

As mentioned in a prior chapter, many gas stations do not have generators. Many operators believe the loss of a few days of business during a storm does not justify the expense. In other words, the private cost of avoiding the risk of a power outage is not enough to warrant preventive or remedial action. This calculation fails to take account of external costs felt by all those who cannot obtain fuel while the gas station is out of service. By not buying generators ahead of time, station owners find themselves unable to provide fuel to their customers, effectively imposing steep, cascading costs on their communities. One way of averting socially paralyzing effects when gas stations have no power is to mandate that gas station owners purchase generators before disasters.

Transparency is the third and final case for government incursion into markets to mitigate risks. When we know what we are buying and with whom we are dealing, we can make the kinds of risk-based judgments about our transactions that enable commerce to thrive. As consumers, we can make informed choices about how to allocate our limited resources. In the same way that markets depend on governments to ensure that contracts are honored, so must they rely upon governments to ensure transparency.

When consumers buy food products or children's toys, they are trusting that these items are safe. When investors purchase a company's stock, they are trusting that the company is keeping honest books and that its stability is as advertised. And when a business asks for a person's identification in order to engage in a transaction, it trusts that the identification documents are authentic and that the person is who he or she purports to be. In each case, transparency absolutely reduces the risk of a bad or dangerous decision.

Simply stated, the global economy depends on trust, and when trust is betrayed, risk increases. In 2008 we saw instances where products imported from overseas contained dangerous ingredients. That not only harms the victims who have used them, but undermines our trust in the whole supply chain relating to these products. The continuing financial crisis was in part a crisis of confidence born out of a concern about lack of transparency regarding the nature of newly created financial products moving through the system. Likewise, when societies cannot trust identification documents due to rising incidents of identity theft, willingness to do business over the Internet, or even face-to-face, falls.

## Striking a Better Balance

The conclusion is clear: What is needed is intelligent, strong, but not overly coercive regulation. The purpose is not to stifle initiative but to ensure that resources are managed and allocated efficiently. However, we must always bear in mind that it is not possible to eradicate all risk.

Put differently, the goal of regulation should be risk management and reduction, not risk elimination. Faced with the risk of airline hijackings, for example, if governments responded by preventing all travelers from boarding planes, that would eliminate hijacking risks, but it would also be doing the work of the terrorists by effectively shutting the airlines down. A risk management or risk reduction strategy entails a far more modest but sensible approach, such as gathering limited commercial information about travelers in order to assess who might pose a potential risk.

Likewise, faced with the risk of terrorists loading shipping containers with deadly explosives, governments could require physical inspection of every incoming container, but that would bring commerce to a grinding halt. A more common-sense approach is to manage the threat by obtaining relevant information about the containers, including their origin, and then assessing which ones pose a higher than average risk of carrying dangerous material. Containers that originate in nations with insecure supply chains would merit closer scrutiny.

While free societies and their governments must avoid the temptations of overregulation through unwise policies trying to eliminate risk, they must not hesitate to regulate and manage in the strategic ways I have outlined. The risks we face are far too serious to be ignored, downplayed, or left to unbounded market forces alone. In the coming years, what is needed are partnerships between governments and the public that embrace the kinds of regulation that facilitate the free market prerogative to make decisions in an intelligent and informed fashion.

Over the last eight years, we have experienced terrorist attacks, natural disasters, and a financial seizure. Each of these carries lessons of risk management. The succession of these crises will tempt some leaders to focus only on the most recent risk, suggesting for example, that we should diminish our focus on natural disasters because we are now occupied with financial risk. But the true lesson of our recent past is that we can ill-afford the luxury of focusing on only the latest example of risk. Our political culture must sustain a capacity to manage all kinds of risks, all at the same time, and without the false promise that risk management means risk elimination.

# Biological Threats and Biodefenses

O NE of the most important priorities for any government is to protect society from lethal threats. Part of that mission necessarily involves guarding against the havoc that biological forces are capable of wreaking on any population.

Such forces can come in the form of pandemics or very serious epidemics—deadly communicable diseases that can ravage communities and potentially threaten the fabric of society. While such diseases have surfaced throughout history in discrete areas of the world, the interdependent, global nature of today's world can facilitate their rapid spread across oceans and continents. This naturally occurring peril is compounded by the fact that the modern wonders of science and technology enable dangerous individuals and groups to harness these potent biological forces, turning them into actual weapons of mass destruction.

While such natural threats as pandemic influenza have yet to reach fully efficient human-to-human transmission, post-9/11 society faces a more immediate, man-made threat from individuals seeking to unleash destruction. In the wake of 9/11, we saw anthrax attacks at home, and we have since seen ricin attacks in other parts of the world. In response to these dangers, we have taken a number of steps to help mitigate at least some of the risk. And, not a moment too soon, our society is finally beginning to think seriously and in a disciplined fashion about how to plan for dealing with a major natural pandemic or biological attack. The challenge is to act decisively and effectively to minimize damage in an environment in which there will be imperfect information and potentially hundreds of thousands, if not millions, of lives lost. The key to meeting the challenge is to approach it in a systematic, comprehensive, unflinching way. We must fully examine the biological threats we face, address the capabilities we must continue to build in order to mitigate them, and consider the complex legal and ethical issues that will arise during a biological calamity if ever we have one. And as emphasized by *World at Risk*, the December 2008 report by the Commission on the Prevention of Weapons of Mass Destruction Proliferation and Terrorism,[1] now is the time to foster a new culture of awareness in response to this deadly risk to our safety and security.

## The Need for Planning

Since a biological outbreak, such as pandemic influenza or a major anthrax attack, is one of the most catastrophic scenarios this country could face, advance planning and preparation are critical. We must work hard today, before disaster strikes, to determine who should be doing what should a disaster happen tomorrow. If we fail to plan, we plan to fail, risking a worst-case outcome. A plan at least provides a running start, as will training and exercising. Planning must involve an understanding of the full dimensions of a public health emergency—natural or man-made. Inevitably, each profession views calamity through the lenses of its own discipline. Thus, medical and public health personnel seek to cure, vaccinate, and alleviate suffering. Yet that is only one part of what must be done during such a crisis.

A biologically induced catastrophe could affect every aspect of society. Issues of scarcity could develop, from emergency room capacity to distribution of medicine. Beyond that, absenteeism across the economy could ensue because of the number of people who would become ill, fear exposure to illness, or stay home with their children if schools closed. When enough people stay home, then without a plan, the power plants cannot run and food will not arrive in supermarkets, which could be closed if no one is there to open them. The results could be cascading problems producing a ripple effect across society, magnifying the damage already inflicted by the underlying disaster.

Compounding these difficulties is the fact that biological disasters arrive not with a bang but a whimper. It can be hours or days before the full impact begins to dawn on society. Moreover, our ability to study or predict the course of the epidemic or pandemic will depend profoundly on how accurate we are in deciding whether it is a natural or a man-made incident. Our public health models presume we know how ordinary diseases spread and circulate. But if a person is carrying an aerosol tank, spraying it in different locales, such behavior will confound the model. Correctly determining whether the problem is natural or manmade is essential. Finally, since a biological event would not typically involve an explosion, it would not be initially experienced by most people as dramatic.

To sum up, if our society continues to avoid sufficient planning, training, exercising, and stockpiling in response to this threat, then if we are ever faced with an efficient human-to-human transmission of pandemic flu or a full-scale anthrax attack, we will not have time to deal with it. If there is one lesson that the years since 9/11 should have taught, it is that advance planning is the only way to respond to a major threat to safety and security. This is certainly true regarding the threats posed by the prospect of naturally occurring contagious diseases migrating here and proliferating. It is at least equally true with respect to the risk of biological agents being weaponized and circulated by terrorists.

In the late 1990s, Al Qaeda began to focus on developing a biological weapons program. After the invasion of Afghanistan, the U.S. government determined that there was a low-tech facility in Kandahar that was aimed at producing anthrax as a weapon. Fortunately, the United States disrupted that laboratory. Moreover, ejecting Al Qaeda from safe havens made it harder for its members to convert chemical or biological substances into weapons of mass destruction. But the increasing development of safe havens along Pakistan's border with Afghanistan and elsewhere is worrisome precisely because they can become sites for reconstituted laboratories for weaponization.

Moreover, Al Qaeda has made it clear that it has no moral qualms about using such weapons once they are made. In 2002, it claimed a moral license to kill millions of Americans in response to imagined mistreatment by the West, and it has since reiterated that claim.[2] Given its barbaric use of weaponry it already possesses, there is no reason to believe that Al Qaeda would not use chemical and biological weaponry—such as aerosolized anthrax, our chief bioterrorism concern—given the opportunity and a fully developed capability.

## A Strategy

So what is our strategy for dealing with these dangers? It is based on Homeland Security Presidential Directive HSPD-10, "Biodefense for the Twenty-First Century," a 2004 order that identifies three key areas of focus: threat awareness and detection, prevention and protection, and response and recovery.

Threat awareness addresses the need to identify and, if possible, incapacitate a threat before it occurs. In the case of pandemic flu, this means identifying and addressing a problem area affected by a possible mutation that allows human-to-human transmission so the threat can be contained. The dilemma arises when other countries fail to disclose that they have a problem area, fearing it would harm their ability to travel and conduct business across the globe. That is why, in order to detect such areas, we must be prepared to deploy our intelligence tools.

This is all the more true if the threat is man-made. Thus, when it comes to threat awareness, we have to operate on a number of levels.

First, we must search for signs of laboratories across the globe that could be poised to weaponize materials. This requires old-fashioned intelligence work, so we can get the information we need to determine if there is a biological attack being planned against us or our allies. In a very real way, intelligence is a critical element in promoting public health in the twenty-first century.

The value of this kind of intelligence was vividly demonstrated in London in spring 2008, at the trial of those suspected of plotting to blow up transatlantic airliners in 2006. Based on diligent intelligence gathering, we learned about the elaborate efforts made to manufacture explosive devices concealed in sports drink bottles.

There simply is no adequate substitute for good intelligence that can help us detect the initial emergence of dangerous biological pathogens or their appearance in our country. For the 91 million people who come to the United States by air and the 411 million who arrive by land each year, we can screen for incoming nuclear or radiological devices, but it is pure fantasy to imagine medically testing all of them as well.

Of course, if we have reason to believe there is illness afoot, then we can begin testing some individuals. If we had credible information about a pandemic brewing elsewhere in the world, we could redirect flights and aircraft from the affected region and screen their passengers more intensively. So screening can be of value, but not without the intelligence that lets us focus on those individuals who might pose a genuine risk.

In other words, to a large degree, detection depends on intelligence. And when it comes to countering biological threats, speed of detection is crucial. It enables us to discover the dimensions of the problem and prepare an efficacious response. A delay of just one day in detecting an anthrax release would delay treatment accordingly, triggering thousands of deaths. To ensure detection, we need to fuse three types of information. One is traditional clinical data. That means relying on the public health community to gather information about people with symptoms that could suggest the presence of something like anthrax or a plague. The problem with this information alone is that by the time symptoms appear, society is already behind the curve. The disease is already upon us.

A second type of information is available to supplement these data. This information concerns pathogens in the air itself. Fortunately, the program called BioWatch, an environmental early detection system, uses air samplers in more than 30 urban areas around the country to help locate and warn of the presence of airborne pathogens.

The final type of information we use to facilitate detection is nonmedical intelligence about enemy threats. For example, a little over a year ago, a case was reported from a hospital that appeared to involve anthrax. We were able to determine that the patient had traveled from a part of the world where anthrax occurs naturally on the skin, and so the matter was resolved and the patient treated.

But let us suppose that in addition to obtaining that clinical information, we had received intelligence that terrorists were about to launch an anthrax attack against the United States. That information would have immediately altered our approach to the patient. We probably would have surged biological detection capability into the area to see whether there was evidence of anthrax spores. And then our ability to use detection tools on location and across the nation would have come into play, enabling us quickly to characterize the nature of the incident and formulate our response.

To integrate these three types of information—clinical, detection, and nonmedical intelligence information—we have created a first-of-its-kind national biosurveillance integration center, a 24/7 operation that opened on 30 September 2008. By fusing clinical data, regular intelligence information, and ultimately BioWatch data, including next generation sensors, we can ensure that decision-makers have an early, immediate, and comprehensive picture of the kind of pathogens that are out there so they can characterize them.

Besides threat awareness and detection, the second of our three areas of focus in dealing with biological threats concerns protection. As we respond to a medical threat, we must work with the business community and use some of the government's tools to prevent disruption in food, water, the power supply, and other necessities while dealing with the hours, days, or even weeks and months of a pandemic or some comparable biological attack.

Part of this is a planning issue. It involves ensuring close coordination between people who operate critical infrastructure and medical personnel with on-the-ground facts about what constitutes appropriate treatment. It also involves ascertaining the actual fear of contagion and the appropriate countermeasures and restrictions that belong in place to ensure that people can come to work with a minimal risk of contracting an illness.

And finally, in addition to awareness and detection, and prevention and protection, we must address the matter of response and recovery with respect to biological threats. It is clearly a complex undertaking. There is obviously the provision of medical care, which lies within the domain of the public health authorities including HHS. They must not only develop and stockpile medicines and vaccines, but also be able to distribute them. In many ways, we and our state partners would be the arms and legs of that distribution.

In the case of a man-made attack as opposed to a natural occurrence, the Department of Justice would play a critical role. If we believed that people possessing the pathogen were moving around the country, finding and arresting them would be an obvious matter of urgency. The ability to limit the damage and need to respond would be a direct result of our ability to intercept the culprits and prevent their carrying out further attacks.

The Environmental Protection Agency would play a vital role in making sure that once the problem was stabilized, we would understand what was needed to clean up and render the affected area safe for reentry. The Department of Agriculture would ensure there were no untoward effects on our food supply. And the Department of Defense would bolster efforts by supplying personnel to perform critical functions pertaining to security and treatment should a surge be necessary.

This indicates the range of departments that must be integrated, brought together, and coordinated through the interagency system in the event of a biological attack. The paramount goals would be to prevent further damage, steer medical supplies and lifesaving items to people (ideally within 48 hours), and provide the public clear direction so their actions do not make their own situation worse.

And that brings us to the core of what we must do to prepare. We must get people to understand how to evaluate messages in the aftermath of a disaster, what personal preparedness plans they must have in place in terms of medicines and other items that they and their loved ones need, and where to go on the Internet to obtain further information that they and their families may need.

One of our most formidable challenges is how to distribute vaccines or medicines among millions of people in a 48-hour, "make-it-or-break-it" environment. Should we, for example, actually distribute prophylactic medical kits around the country or allow people to purchase those kits for their medicine cabinets? How do we make sure that people do not abuse them?

And then how do we deal with the fact that, in any mass distribution, there will not likely be enough doctors to provide the checkups that normally precede administering pills for the enormous number of potentially affected people within the 48-hour span? Do we distribute medicines given the knowledge that some people will experience negative side effects, in some instances severe? If we believe that taking this risk with a small number of people is justifiable in order to avoid a certain hazard to a far greater number of people, then what is the liability for the manufacturer? Will the manufacturer or distributor be willing to provide medicines if the government cannot assure them that they will not be sued? This is hardly an academic issue. Consider the Foreign Intelligence Surveillance Act issue and what happened to businesses that cooperated in good faith with the government on security matters following the 9/11 attacks.

Simply stated, if government's message to the business community is "cooperate with us during a national emergency, and then when it has passed we will change the rules and hold you liable," then we will get scant cooperation. A possible consequence would be that companies would not distribute enough antibiotics because they would be forced to wait for legal opinions before releasing them. In this case, it would be too late to fix the problem.

In summary, the threats posed by biological material are real enough, and we must confront them with a strategy that is comprehensive and a mindset that is clear-eyed and forward-looking.

## Legal Challenges

I would be remiss if I did not lay out some of the more challenging legal issues that could arise with the onset of a biological catastrophe. As with other aspects of this problem, it is essential that they be discussed and deliberated upon before, not after, a national emergency arises.

Questions concerning such issues as restrictions on movement and how to control infection fall within the jurisdiction of the states. We need to ask whether the federal government should be able to trump the states in these areas. If a New Jersey governor were to decide that due to an outbreak in New York, no New Yorker could come into New Jersey, would that be acceptable? What if that made it harder to track down the perpetrators of the attack, or to ensure that adequate food was reaching the afflicted area?

Should we be able to regulate the bandwidth of our communications during a public health crisis so that employees can telecommute without disrupting the nation's cyber systems? Should we ask broadband providers to restrict access for high-consumption, low-productivity devices such as video games so that we can use the bandwidth for more important things?

What are the limits on government ability to quarantine and isolate? Can people be prevented from doing the twenty-first-century equivalent of shouting fire in a crowded theater, providing deliberate or negligent misinformation on the airwaves that could cause the death of thousands of people who were misled about what to do during a medical emergency?

These are excruciatingly difficult questions with no perfect answers. The more thoughtful deliberation we have about them in advance, the better off we will be.

We must live with the consequences of our answers. If we decide that we must leave matters of quarantine in the hands of the states, we must understand that this will render the federal government incapable of forcing a state to institute a quarantine. Should a day come when a quarantine becomes a medical necessity, it will be too late to turn back the clock and do the decision over.

Returning to the liability issue: if our society is unwilling to hold companies blameless for distributing drugs to protect millions of people during a national emergency, it will do no good to blame them when not enough drugs reach the people who need them. Clearly, the time to have thorough, candid, and public conversations about these issues and trade-offs is today, before anything happens tomorrow. This is true not only of legal matters, but also of every aspect of the threat and how we should respond.

For those who insist that this is fear-mongering about the unthinkable, they need to recall how before the morning of September 11, 2001, it would have seemed unthinkable that we could lose 3,000 American lives in a single day. Preparing by word and deed for the unthinkable is hardly a pleasant exercise, but if we engage in it today, we can prevent far greater harm from befalling us tomorrow. If we plan for the worst, we just might avoid some and maybe even all of it.

# The Question of FEMA and
# Homeland Security

WHILE we have not had a successful terrorist attack launched against us since 9/11, we have experienced major natural disasters in recent years. From wildfires in California and tornados and unprecedented flooding in the Midwest to Hurricanes Gustav and Ike along the Gulf Coast, the nation has faced serious challenges from the unleashing of nature's fury. In each of these instances, the response of the U.S. government in support of stricken states and localities was led by the Federal Emergency Management Agency.

By all accounts, FEMA acquitted itself well. This bears eloquent testimony to its dedicated members who put their lives on the line in order to save the lives of others. It is also a tribute to FEMA's success in solidifying its partnerships with state and local authorities with whom it has planned and worked. And I would contend that it is the result of FEMA members working closely and effectively with their counterparts across the Department of Homeland Security, from Customs and Border Protection (CBP) agents and officers and Transportation Security Agency (TSA) air marshals and screening officials to U.S. Coast Guard members.

In response to Hurricane Ike, for example, CBP provided critical security for transit of life-sustaining goods at commodity distribution locations for FEMA. TSA, in turn, supported 20 FEMA commodity distribution locations in the area of Harris County, Texas, where Houston is situated. TSA fielded 366 of its employees, who assisted FEMA by providing hands and boots to distribute food to people in need. And our Coast Guard helped FEMA's response efforts by performing a myriad of land, sea, and air search-and-rescue missions.

When analyzing the response of FEMA and our other components and offices to recent disasters such as Ike, three lessons can be learned.

First, when it comes to any kind of incident or crisis, planning and preparation remain the essential preconditions for doing a good job. The much-heralded success in evacuating people in advance of Hurricane Gustav was the fruit of years of conscientious planning, training, and exercising with state and local authorities. The value of these activities is that when unexpected events arrive, improvisation can take place, because a foundation has been laid.

The second lesson of these incidents concerns what I call the three Cs of disaster management: cooperation, communication, and coordination. Simply stated, at all levels of government, all three are necessary to ensure the kind of disaster response that saves lives and assists communities.

And finally, at the federal level, I am convinced that the integration of our preparedness and response functions under a single roof—the Department of Homeland Security—remains critical to ensuring a sound, effective response capability for every type of disaster.

---

## Stronger Together Than Separate

It is this final point on which I will elaborate. Since its inception, DHS has gone through a number of congressionally mandated reorganizations. The temptation in the future will be to keep tinkering with the department, impeding its ability to perform its duties with maximum effectiveness. Succumbing to this temptation are those who call for the removal of FEMA from DHS. They maintain that while FEMA is involved with consequence management or incident response, the rest of DHS is charged with preventing and protecting against disasters that necessitate a response. They conclude that since these are separate functions, they belong under separate roofs.

The problem with this argument is that it is not FEMA alone that handles our response to incidents. As we saw with the response efforts to Hurricane Ike, the Coast Guard, CBP, and TSA played supportive but critical roles.

Put another way, the job of Coast Guard members is not only to protect our coastlines from preventable disasters; it also encompasses such activities as search-and-rescue efforts once a disaster has occurred. Their mission is not only about prevention and protection; it is also about preparedness and response.

To enhance overall preparedness, FEMA and other DHS components have endeavored to plan, train, exercise, and build capabilities together in a way that would not be possible were they treated as separate entities rather than operating together under one roof. From terrorism to hurricanes, it should be clear that "stovepiping" is inimical to efficient, effective, lifesaving responses. Clearly, the ability to prepare together is a function of our ability to be integrated together. Thus a key reason for FEMA to remain in DHS is that it strengthens the nation's incident preparedness by facilitating cooperation among organizations that share preparedness and response missions.

A second reason is that once an incident occurs, responding to it is easier if these agencies are under the same umbrella. If FEMA were its own department outside of DHS, rather than one of its key components, then calling on a DHS agency for assistance would be more time-consuming. It would involve the formal process of one independent department requesting the help of another. But with FEMA inside DHS, the DHS secretary could respond by instantly putting every departmental element and capability at FEMA's disposal.

This ability to act quickly is vital when lives hang in the balance. Citing FEMA's successful response to the 2008 natural disasters, U.S. Senate Homeland Security Committee chairman Senator Joe Lieberman and ranking member Senator Susan Collins wrote the following words in a joint letter published in the *New York Times* in December 2008: "Lives are saved when skills, resources and missions are united—not dispersed."[1] This is a lesson our country has learned well in national security. When the Department of Defense was first created after World War II, none of its current components wanted to be in it. Each component, from the Army to the Marine Corps, viewed it as a diminution of its traditional prerogative as a stand-alone department. Each resisted the full integration of the Defense Department through the late 1970s, when the consequence was Desert 1, the tragically failed attempt to rescue American diplomats held hostage by revolutionaries in Iran. This led to the passage of Goldwater-Nichols Act a decade later, which brought further institutional integration.

A final reason for keeping FEMA in DHS is that, while FEMA could respond by itself to certain natural disaster scenarios, this would hardly be the case regarding a man-made disaster like a major terrorist attack. In order to respond successfully to a dirty bomb or biological attack, FEMA would almost certainly require the counterterrorism capabilities of DHS in the arena of information and intelligence. To fulfill its responsibilities, FEMA must continue to be a consumer of the kind of intelligence and expertise that the entire Department of Homeland Security brings to the issue of combating terrorism.

## The Stronger Model

In short, it is clear that if we want FEMA to do its job best, we must ensure that it remains a part of the department. But while FEMA needs DHS in order to fulfill its mission, it is equally evident that DHS needs FEMA, and for exactly the same reason. To fulfill its homeland security mission—one that includes preparedness and response as well as prevention and protection—DHS must continue to include the nation's leading emergency management agency.

This point is a critical one, for it reminds us that as the Department of Homeland Security was created, it was shaped in accordance with a specific presidential directive—Homeland Security Presidential Directive 5 (HSPD-5)[2] —that envisioned precisely this kind of comprehensive, across-the-board mission of incident management, one that cuts across agency lines and has national implications.

Essentially, HSPD-5 made the secretary of homeland security the nation's operational incident manager in the event of a terrorist strike or natural disaster of significant consequence. The purpose was to recognize that while the White House guides policy, the operational planning, training and execution must be housed in a specific cabinet level department, one that is charged with ensuring that all of the nation's relevant operational components were being synchronized and working well together.

This incident management system, which has been adopted by a number of states across the nation, recognizes that when dealing with a potential terrorist strike, for example, we must look simultaneously at how to prevent further attacks, how to protect against attacks that are under way, and how to respond to and mitigate the attacks that have already taken place. If these elements are not brought together, the result will be a disjointed response that costs lives and makes a bad situation all the more tragic.

Without an incident manager, the result can be what transpired in November 2008 in Mumbai, India, where a lack of coordination and communication between agencies—between emergency responders and law enforcement and military personnel—plagued efforts to deal with the aftermath of a terrorist attack.

With an incident manager, we can have a properly coordinated response on an operational basis. In July 2006, for example, during the war between Hezbollah and Israel in Lebanon, there were questions raised about the safety of Americans living in Lebanon. Working through CBP and TSA and with the State Department, DHS was able to apply this incident management construct to help repatriate those Americans, removing them from harm's way.

A month later, in August 2006, when a plot directed at flights from Britain to the United States was revealed, we worked through TSA and CBP and with the State and Defense Departments. Within eight hours, we transformed the way America deals with flights and airline security in order to prevent any element of the uncovered plot from coming to fruition.

Less than a year later, in June 2007, we had two successive emergencies that were resolved through incident management. One turned out to be an unfounded scare that foot-and-mouth disease— a potentially calamitous livestock plague—had entered the United States through infected swine. DHS and its components worked with the Departments of Agriculture and Health and Human Services, the FBI, and the National Counterterrorism Center to assess immediately whether this was a terrorist incident, develop a common situational picture of what was happening, and swiftly determine that the matter was not a threat. Had it been a threat, we would have instituted certain protocols at the border and certain medical protocols that would have mitigated the damage.

A day after we resolved that problem, we were confronted by the terrorist attacks against Britain in London and Glasgow, culminating in the effort to blow up Glasgow's airport. Once again, we were able to coordinate a response with CBP, TSA, and other elements of national power.

In each of these instances, we were able, using the incident management model, to bring together different organizations precisely in the coordinated way that was contemplated by those who helped found the Department of Homeland Security.

As we look ahead to future challenges, I am convinced that this model is the right one on which to build. It is the best possible model for reducing the risk to our nation and its people at every point along the safety-and-security continuum. If our aim is to maximize prevention and protection, preparedness and response, we now have a firm foundation in place. Clearly, it is not a fully constructed or polished structure. It is, however, the basic architecture. I am hopeful that my successors will continue to strengthen and elaborate on this structure in a way that will ultimately make America safer.

No disaster is ever going to be painless and easy. That is why they are called disasters. But we can make them much less difficult and costly and, most important, far less deadly. If the recent past is prologue, we have already begun doing so. There is every reason to believe that in the coming years, if they do not discard the model, my successors will continue to improve our ability to respond quickly, effectively, and in a coordinated fashion.

# INTERNATIONAL DIMENSIONS

# 14

# Cooperation and Consensus Abroad

A CURIOUS notion has emerged about how the United States has tried to navigate the seas of global security since the September 11 terrorist attacks. It depicts Washington as charting a solitary course characterized by premises, principles, and policies that diverge dramatically from those of other nations—notably its European allies.

This notion is false and also misleading about the trend of developments. I can attest to the realities based on my extensive interactions with my security counterparts in Europe and elsewhere. Differences in approach do exist, largely rooted in culture, geography and history. But their importance and weight have been exaggerated and are now declining in practice. What I have witnessed is a growing convergence among nations—especially among our transatlantic partners—in the battle against terrorism. I see a common recognition of the terrorist threat, a shared vision for an effective response to it and an evolving consensus on the specific steps that are needed now.

Most nations, including those of Europe, clearly grasp the danger that terrorism poses to their safety. More than that, they understand that the threat we face is not merely that of terrorism, which is simply a tactic, but one of ideology. This was put well by Peter Clarke, who heads counterterrorism for Scotland Yard. "The current terrorist threat is of such a scale and intractability that we must not only defeat [those] who plot and carry out appalling acts of violence. We must also find a way of defeating the ideas that drive them."[1]

When the Taliban were Osama bin Laden's handmaidens in ruling Afghanistan, the outcome provided a revealing portrait of the kind of ideas the terrorists embrace. While in power, they destroyed the works of other religions. They tortured and murdered those who transgressed their rigid rules governing every detail of life. They compelled women to become the virtual property of their fathers or husbands, denying them the right to own property, get an education or otherwise determine their own destinies.

Their dreams of domination may appear ridiculously grandiose, but our experience of fascism and communism instructs us never to underestimate the power of determined fanatics to fulfill their ambitions. Moreover, in the Middle East, North Africa, and South Asia, the extremists have already been able to seize territory within failing states, creating their own statelets in which they rule. Equally important, they are aided by the latest technology and by the forces of globalization, which empower them to carry out the kinds of activities that only large armies could once do. The threat we face is shared not only by transatlantic democracies but by leaders around the world.

Of course, it is one thing to agree broadly on the nature of the danger we confront from ideologically driven terrorism but quite another to concur on how to combat it. Yet here, too, we see the unmistakable outlines of a global consensus. Around the world, governments are arriving at three important realizations on how best to build a strategy to defend our countries, our people, and our way of life.

First, they are starting to see that in order to protect themselves, they must not only operate within their own borders and ports of entry, but beyond them as well. To a growing extent, they recognize the need to extend their security perimeters so they can stop dangerous people abroad before they end up on planes heading for our homelands. Second, since this strategy requires working with other countries, nations are coming to see that they cannot pursue the business of security alone. Strong partnerships among countries are essential. And finally, nations are coming to agree that while security measures must be taken abroad as well as at home and in concert with others, no nation or group of nations can be everywhere at once.

The quest to eliminate all risk is quixotic, so nations are attempting instead to *manage* it. It is worth adding that any country that consistently pursues risk elimination will end up harming what it is attempting to protect. In short, governments are concurring not only on the nature of the terrorist threat but on a broad strategy to stop bad individuals from attacking the people and infrastructure in our respective countries.

Unquestionably, this strategy has its challenges. For example, in America, each year we welcome more than 400 million travelers—91 million by air. The good news is that only a tiny handful might pose a genuine threat; the bad news is that, given modern technology, it only takes a few to wreak untold havoc. While we have terrorist watch lists that identify people we know to be dangerous, we need to find individuals who are terrorists but are not yet known to us.

The question is how best to do it without taking the kinds of draconian measures that would shut down travel altogether.

In the United States, we are confronting this challenge by focusing on three key areas: information, biometrics, and secure documentation. By collecting just a few key pieces of nonsensitive, commercial information, we can identify the small number of passengers who warrant a closer look before they board a plane or enter our country. In 2007 this approach took a giant step forward with our agreement with the European Union, in which the EU agreed to transfer passenger name record (PNR) data to DHS from air carriers operating transatlantic flights.

Even before this transatlantic agreement was reached, data of this sort had proved to be a useful tool for combating terrorism. In April 2006 at Boston's Logan Airport, two arriving passengers exhibited travel patterns indicating "high-risk behaviors," and so Customs and Border Protection (CBP) officers decided to take a closer look at them. In the "secondary interview" process, one subject stated that he was traveling to America on business for a group suspected of having financial ties to Al Qaeda. When his baggage was examined, officers discovered images of armed men, one of them labeled "Mujahadin." Both passengers were refused entry to the United States.

Three years earlier, on the basis of such data and other analytics, an inspector at Chicago's O'Hare Airport pulled aside an individual for secondary questioning. When his answers did not satisfy the security officers, he was denied entry into the United States—but not before his fingerprints had been taken. The next time we saw those fingerprints or rather parts of them, they were on the steering wheel of a suicide vehicle that blew up and killed 32 people in Iraq.

The use of fingerprinting and other biometrics is a second way of picking out terrorists from the mass of innocent travelers and laying the basis for identifying more of them. Under the US-VISIT program, visitors arriving at our ports of entry have had their two index fingers scanned and then compared with the fingerprints in databases from prior entries or with their visa records. The procedure verifies a visitor's identity and ensures that the person is not a known felon or terrorist.

The chances of success are improved by taking prints of all 10 fingers. We are in a process of transition to a 10-fingerprint screening program at our ports of entry, and this will increase our capability for finding matches with latent prints that have been collected from battlefields, safe houses, and training camps around the world. A terrorist can no longer escape notice just because we do not have a match with an index finger. The practice of 10-fingerprint collection will have a deterrent effect on visa applicants who know that they have left prints in terrorist locales that may now be in Western records.

Besides PNR and our 10-fingerprint initiative, a third example of how we will locate dangerous individuals among the vast throngs of visitors to the United States is our attempts to unmask terrorists pretending to be someone else. For this purpose, we are counting on a new requirement for travelers to present secure identification documents—a program known as the Western Hemisphere Travel Initiative (WHTI). It establishes documentation requirements for previously exempt travelers entering the United States. As a first step, in January 2007 we implemented a new requirement for U.S. citizens, together with citizens of Canada and Bermuda, to present passports when they fly into the United States from points of departure within the Western Hemisphere.

This step toward standardized, secure, and reliable documentation will enable border officials to identify travelers quickly, reliably, and accurately at ports. Until now, the security risk has been aggravated by allowing travelers of this sort to use approximately 8,000 types of identification. That practice made it difficult to assess travelers seeking entry without significantly slowing the time required to process their paperwork. By limiting and standardizing the documentation requirement, WHTI aims to facilitate the process while enhancing border security.

The next step was implemented in January 2008, when the United States ended the practice of accepting oral declarations of citizenship alone as a basis for access from citizens of neighboring countries and our own at our land and sea ports of entry.

Critics have cited all three of these initiatives—PNR data collection and usage, biometrics, and secure traveler identification—as evidence that the United States is grabbing every available piece of information, acting like a Big Brother on the world stage. In fact, similar programs are being implemented by governments around the world, especially in nations which share our democratic values and traditions, including the value of privacy. Prominent among them are our friends and partners across the Atlantic. In February 2008, the EU proposed a biometric entry/exit system that resembles our US-VISIT program. And in November 2007, the EU released a proposed requirement for its member states that mirrors our own PNR data-usage rules in border-management processes.

As for individual countries, the United Kingdom has embarked on a seven-year initiative, known as the "eBorders program," to establish an integrated biometric and biographic border-management system. Ireland will roll out a similar program to secure its common area with the UK. The Netherlands, Portugal, Germany, Britain, and Malaysia have all pioneered expedited entry or registered traveler programs to allow pre-approved travelers to move quickly through passport control. For years, Australia has run an Electronic Travel Authorization program that mitigates risk thanks to an automated screening program that verifies the eligibility of would-be visitors. Japan has begun recording the fingerprints and photographs of all foreign visitors in a manner compatible with the US-VISIT concept.

As the *Economist* put it in November 2007, "*all* countries are moving towards the collection of 'biometric' information" (emphasis added).[2] Although the article focused on Japan, it underscored evidence from around the world of convergence among countries on security matters arising from the terrorist threat. And when it comes to our transatlantic partnerships, American and European cooperation in combating terrorism deepens every year, a trend evidenced by the dismantled plots in Germany, Denmark, and the UK in 2007 alone.

Terrorism poses a continuing challenge, including its practitioners' ability to adapt to security countermeasures. Hence we must do everything possible to preserve and strengthen this partnership between the United States and Europe—a partnership that won the Cold War and one that has been remarkably successful thus far in disrupting the plots of our common foes.

We have come a very long way in dealing with the terrorist danger that threatens us all. The threat, however, remains. We owe it to those who depend on us not to grow complacent and fail in our duty to protect them, but to build on the progress we have made and the consensus we have achieved.

# 15

# The Responsibility
# to Contain

As economies, societies, and cultures have become increasingly interconnected, the traditional conception of threats to security as stemming from identifiable sources in individual countries has become antiquated. Today, many threats are stateless in origin and transnational in scope. Terrorist groups such as Hezbollah and Al Qaeda have cells in multiple countries, often operating without the active support of any government but still capable of committing attacks with global impact. Both 9/11 and the unsuccessful plot to blow up airliners over the Atlantic Ocean in 2006 were aimed at disrupting the global air transportation network. Potentially crippling attacks on the power grid or financial institutions could come from a computer anywhere in the world.

Fighting elusive and transnational enemies that do not respect the traditional conventions of warfare requires international cooperation. Terrorists are unlike past enemies of the United States. Whereas the Soviet Union had a defined territory with infrastructure and resources that could be targeted in retaliation for any aggression committed against the United States, terrorist groups have no established boundaries. A strategy of deterrence through threats of retaliation would prove ineffective against terrorists, since so many are willing to die for their cause. Moreover, they often strike at global or transnational targets, seeking to exploit the seams between national jurisdictions, where enforcement may be shared, ambiguous, or inconsistent.

In light of these developments, the field of international law is taking on greater relevance. Since 9/11, it has been central to discussions about the "war on terror," on issues ranging from the treatment of enemy combatants to the standards of security that should apply to global trade and travel. Unfortunately, just as international law is becoming more relevant, its objectivity is becoming more questionable. Some in the international legal community see international law as a means for advancing political agendas against the United States rather than as a valuable tool for addressing increasingly global concerns. Employing the rhetoric of international law, critics of the United States have challenged everything from its foreign and homeland security policies to its enforcement of purely domestic laws. In recent years, international lawyers and scholars have sought to subordinate established U.S. laws and even U.S. constitutional provisions to international legal mandates and "customary" international law—in which "custom" is not traditionally interpreted, as being based on the actual practices of states, but instead is dictated by the policy preferences of foreign judges or, worse yet, international scholars and academics.

The concept of a global legal order—launched by sober-minded leaders such as Woodrow Wilson, Franklin Roosevelt, and Winston Churchill—is often exploited by ideologues and antagonists of the

United States who are bent on waging "lawfare" against U.S. interests. As a result, some critics have argued that the most prudent course for the United States is to opt out of international legal institutions whenever possible. Yet a wholesale rejection of international law would mean surrendering the field of intellectual combat to those who see international law mainly as an instrument to constrain the United States. And more important, it would risk sacrificing real opportunities to move international law in a direction that promotes the many interests that the United States shares with the rest of the world.

Building a better international legal regime is a task U.S. legal thinkers and policymakers should embrace. To do so, they must first define the proper scope of international law. This modern international legal order must be predicated on a new principle, under which individual states assume reciprocal obligations to contain transnational threats emerging from within their borders so as to prevent them from infringing on the peace and safety of fellow states around the world. This framework will be successful only if the sovereign consent of individual nations remains the bedrock of international law and only if it resists the trend within international legal circles to forcibly impose broad and abstract legal norms through nondemocratic means.

## The Centrality of Consent

The typical strategy of international legal activists today is to challenge the idea of national sovereignty. This is a revolutionary tactic, particularly because sovereignty has played an important role in the development of the international system for over three centuries. Under the Westphalian model of sovereignty—which dates back to 1648—an independent state is not subject to external control over its internal affairs without its consent. For democratic nations in today's world, consent has added significance. Democracy is based on the principle that the people are sovereign and that only with their consent may a government rule with legitimacy. Democratic national sovereignty therefore reflects the ideal that citizens should be governed only by laws to which they have assented. Imposing international legal mandates on a nation without its consent undermines this traditional concept of sovereignty and conflicts with the democratic will. For this reason, international law has often been based on the consent of nations by way of treaties, in which nations voluntarily agree to abide by certain rules, or through customary international law, which infers tacit consent through widespread state practice. To be sure, not all sources of international law are explicitly based on sovereign consent. So-called peremptory norms, or *jus cogens* norms, are rules—such as those forbidding slavery or genocide—considered to be so deeply embedded in international law that they bind all nations, even absent national consent.

An international legal framework founded on a consent-based model of sovereignty is advantageous for several reasons. By requiring the explicit or implicit consent of nations before a particular international standard binds them, this approach gains the legitimacy that democratic legal traditions and processes provide. Consent-based international law also allows states to protect their own critical interests by bargaining for or withholding consent from certain provisions of a treaty. Finally, grounding international law in consent acknowledges national differences in culture and legal philosophy by ensuring that international rules fit within an international consensus—one shared by real governments, not merely endorsed by intellectual elites. Academics, lawyers, and judges who challenge the continued relevance of consent in international law often treat "sovereignty" as a pejorative term or an antiquated concept. Many of these critics depart from the traditional view of international law as consisting primarily of reciprocal obligations among nations. For example, some have argued in particular cases that international agreements automatically confer legal rights on individuals that may be enforced directly without state support or even against the laws of the individuals' own countries. And some further argue that international law is not limited to what is agreed on by nations in treaties or accepted through widespread practice but also encompasses a set of standards based on highly general and "evolving" universal principles. For example, international legal scholar Philippe Sands argues that "to claim that states are as sovereign today as they were fifty years ago is to ignore reality."[1] Sands describes international law as a set of obligations that "take on a logic and a life of their own" and that "do not stay within the neat boundaries that states thought they were creating when they were negotiated." Late Harvard Law School professor Louis Sohn went even farther in unmooring international law from consent, positing that "states really never make international law on the subject of human rights. It is made by the people that care, the professors, the writers of textbooks and casebooks, and the authors of articles in leading international law journals."[2] Even conservative commentator Robert Kagan has called on U.S. policymakers to "welcome a world of pooled and diminished national sovereignty," arguing that the United States "has little to fear and much to gain in a world of expanding laws and norms based on liberal ideals and designed to protect them."[3]

Of course, not all who seek to diminish the role of sovereignty in the development of international law are so explicit. International legal jurists and scholars often purport to recognize sovereign consent as the foundation of international obligations but then proceed to "identify" and apply norms or principles of customary international law that are not evidenced by actual state practice. For example, a court may proclaim that there is a rule that prohibits particular government actions without considering whether most nations indeed adhere to that rule. Alarmingly, some jurists rely for support

on academics and commentators who do not merely catalog international law but rather seek to influence its development according to
their own policy preferences. It makes no practical difference that
these jurists may pay lip service to the importance of sovereignty;
the effect of their efforts is to undermine nations' prerogative to
choose their own laws.

Whether invoked explicitly or implicitly, the most common jus-
tifications for rejecting sovereign consent as the foundation of international law are flawed. One argument is that the growing global
activity among nations creates the need for more comprehensive
systems of international law to govern global conduct. This need,
however, does not justify eliminating sovereign consent as the basis
for imposing international obligations. Indeed, requiring the consent of nations has not prevented the international community from
addressing a host of substantive issues, ranging from trade to arms
control to endangered species protection. Moreover, individuals
still principally identify themselves as part of a particular national
community and resist decisions imposed on them by foreign actors
and institutions without their consent. A visible case in point was
the rejection of the European Constitution by voters in France and
the Netherlands in 2005 and the more recent rejection of the Lis-
bon Treaty by voters in Ireland in 2008. Another objection to sovereign consent holds that all humans possess certain fundamental
rights that cannot be denied, even by the consent of the majority.
But the recognition of fundamental human rights raises the harder
and more particular question of how those rights should be defined
and applied, and by whom. Bodies such as the United Nations include member states that often do not share a common position and
whose values often clash with those of the United States and other
democratic states. For example, the UN Human Rights Council has
passed resolutions urging states to adopt laws combating the "defa-
mation of religions,"[4] which would prohibit the type of open dis-

cussion about religious and political matters that is protected under the First Amendment to the U.S. Constitution. The UN also held a conference to examine gun control provisions, ones that would be at odds with the Second Amendment, and in 2008 the UN General Assembly passed a resolution calling for a moratorium on capital punishment with "a view to abolishing the death penalty," even though the U.S. Supreme Court has repeatedly upheld it. Ironically, many of the states supporting such initiatives have a poor record when it comes to respecting the rights of their own citizens.

In short, absent an express treaty or convention, giving international bodies the power to decide what are new and expanded fundamental rights would allow countries to advance nationalist or bloc political agendas under the guise of human rights. It would also empower an often self-perpetuating international legal establishment—courts, advocates, academics, and activists—to "discover" international human rights by relying selectively on transnational agreements that may express only regional consensus or by drawing on philosophical or academic texts that reflect particular intellectual fashions. Such amorphous sources provide questionable grounds for mandatory international obligations.

Nevertheless, international courts have been receptive to arguments based on abstract principles that serve to erode the consensual foundation of international rules. One such example is the 1986 decision of the International Court of Justice in the case *Nicaragua v. United States*. In that case, Nicaragua filed suit against the United States under several multilateral treaties. The United States, however, had explicitly limited its consent to ICJ jurisdiction to when all signatories that would be affected by the court's decision were parties to the case in question. It therefore asserted that the ICJ lacked jurisdiction over this case, in part because of the absence of other signatories. Although the ICJ recognized that it lacked jurisdiction to resolve the dispute under the relevant treaty provisions, it avoided these limitations entirely by finding that such obligations "retain a separate existence" as part of customary international law. The ICJ found the United States liable under these international norms.

Another example of the emerging tendency of international jurists to subordinate national sovereignty to subjective and sometimes ill-fitting principles of international law is the 2004 ICJ advisory opinion that questioned the legality of a barrier constructed by Israel to prevent terrorists from entering its territory. In support of the barrier, Israel invoked Article 51 of the UN Charter, which allows countries to defend themselves against armed attacks. The ICJ, however, concluded that Article 51 recognizes an inherent right of self-defense only in the event of an attack "by one State against another State." Even though it recognized that "Israel has to face numerous indiscriminate and deadly acts of violence against its civilian population," the ICJ relied on a narrow reading of the UN Charter to reject a fundamental attribute of state sovereignty—a country's right to protect its citizens. September 11 and subsequent terrorist attacks make a narrow reading of Article 51 seem out of date.

Fortunately, the U.S. Supreme Court has been less receptive than the ICJ to the argument that international law creates enforceable legal obligations without consent. In recent cases, the Court has held that U.S. treaty obligations may not always take precedence over domestic legal rules and procedures and that international treaty obligations are diplomatic commitments that generally do not become binding domestic law without the explicit consent of Congress.

In the past, U.S. policymakers have reacted to the shift away from consent-based international law by limiting U.S. involvement in international legal institutions. Notably, the U.S. government responded to the establishment of the International Criminal Court by prohibiting military and financial aid to countries that recognized its jurisdiction. It did so out of concern that such recognition could subject U.S. military personnel to prosecution before international judges.

## In Defense of International Law

Americans are understandably troubled when international law is misused as a tool to target the United States. But if the United States responds by withdrawing from international legal institutions in order to protect its national interests, everyone will lose. The international community will lose the cooperation of a global superpower, whose resources are often necessary for any meaningful enforcement of global standards, and the United States will lose the support of other nations. Moreover, if the United States responds to flawed international rulings by abandoning the idea of international law, it will undermine its efforts to project "soft power," an important tool of U.S. foreign policy.

Given that international law is an inescapable fixture in today's global political landscape, there is a better way to address modern legal activism. International law should be neither a political tool used to undermine the sovereignty of individual states nor an instrument used by those who seek shelter behind the sovereignty of one country to launch attacks against another.

A modern, consent-based system of international law will be most effective and widely accepted if it is predicated on a clear set of twenty-first-century containment principles that reflect modern obligations of reciprocal sovereignty. These principles would recognize that each state has the inherent autonomy to regulate its own internal security affairs. At the same time, each sovereign nation must respect the sovereignty of other nations, so that all nations are obliged to contain the external consequences of any security threats emerging from within their own borders. This is similar to the legal principle of nuisance: that a property owner has an obligation to stop any activity on his or her property that substantially infringes on the well-being of his or her neighbors. In particular, individual states must take reasonable measures to contain the potentially destructive consequences of these security threats to prevent them from spreading and interfering with other states' sovereign right to exclusive authority over their territories. And when countries fail to live up to this responsibility, international law should recognize—and indeed authorize—mechanisms that would allow protective action on the part of the world community and, if necessary, the injured or threatened states. Such a framework would reflect the libertarian notion that the prerogative of a state not to provide security extends only so far as its choices do not actively threaten the security of other states.

Implicit in this new reciprocal containment principle are three fundamental ideas. The first is that under long-applied Westphalian principles of sovereignty, the methods by which a nation chooses to protect its own citizens from internal, nonstate threats, such as terrorism or crime, are primarily a domestic matter that falls largely outside the purview of international law. This is so because governments—and especially democratic governments—are accountable and responsive to their own citizens, as opposed to the citizens or governments of other states.

Second, international law can play a central role in establishing mechanisms to secure global or transnational institutions and activities, such as international travel, finance, and trade. In these areas, national law lacks the jurisdictional reach to address threats to the integrity of global systems—for example, piracy in international waters or attacks on international flights. Only international rules that synchronize enforcement efforts across nations can prevent terrorists from exploiting vulnerabilities in the seams between nations' legal systems.

Third, when one country harbors terrorists or other dangerous actors, international law must acknowledge that such a nation has an obligation to avoid becoming a platform for attacks on other sovereign nations. Today, the security of the international system is increasingly characterized by interdependence. On matters from nuclear terrorism to cybersecurity to bioterrorism, the failure to secure a single node of the global security network can threaten to undermine the entire system. Unlike during past eras, the most serious threats to sovereignty today do not necessarily come from the official acts of other states; rather, they come from other states' unwillingness or inability to act to contain deadly nonstate threats that develop within their borders. It would be misguided to view such decisions merely as exercises of inviolable "sovereign authority." Instead, they should be viewed as imperiling the sovereignty of those nations that find themselves at the receiving end of dangerous nonstate threats.

A new international legal framework that confronts modern threats is long overdue. Despite the novel legal challenges raised by the spread of terrorism, the tendency has been to debate global security issues within the confines of existing, and largely outdated, international legal frameworks. Implementing an international order that advances U.S. security interests will require difficult decisions and sustained work for at least a generation. To begin, the United States and its partners must ground the reciprocal responsibility to contain threats on three core principles: nonsubordination, collaborative security, and reciprocal sovereignty.

## A Nonsubordinate Domain

First and foremost, a containment framework for international law must avoid subordinating consent-based domestic security measures to foreign norms. The ability of a state to control its internal affairs, including its domestic laws, is a core aspect of national sovereignty.

Nations' legal systems—even those of established democracies—differ markedly from one another in how they deal with domestic crime and terrorism. For example, the United States and European countries differ on the permissibility of the death penalty, the ability of prosecutors to seek plea bargains, the requirements for judicial authorization to conduct surveillance, and the use of an adversarial, as opposed to an inquisitorial, trial process. Because these features reflect the cultural and political attributes of particular countries on matters affecting individuals within their own sovereign territories, they are not appropriate subjects for international lawmaking. International law has no business interfering with the U.S. domestic system of justice; by the same token, the United States should respect fundamentally fair domestic systems of law that may yet differ from its own. Accordingly, the United States should be particularly averse to efforts that invoke vague or untested foreign principles to override measures adopted democratically by sovereign governments.

Indeed, abandoning consent-based domestic rules in favor of transnational norms is especially unjustified when the particular norm involved would imperil a state's ability to protect the security of its own citizens. Liberty-respecting democracies will inevitably strike different balances when they weigh important security objectives against competing considerations such as privacy or economic development. International law will undermine its own legitimacy if it forces individual countries to adopt risks that they have specifically sought to avoid through reasonable, democratically enacted policies.

Consider, for example, the invocation of *jus cogens*. Traditionally, such peremptory norms have prohibited only truly egregious domestic acts. But international activists and legal advocates are increasingly seeking the recognition of new peremptory norms that would invalidate domestic laws and policies. For example, lawyers have argued in past federal litigation that *jus cogens* norms forbid imposing the death penalty and that they limit immigration officials' authority to detain deportable criminal aliens whose home countries will not accept them. Several scholars have gone even further, concluding that peremptory norms should confer additional rights, including the "right to unionize." Although such rights may be worthy of protection and may even be recognized under U.S. law, invoking international law in this way is troubling because it circumvents democratic domestic laws, safeguards, and processes. And the more that courts and scholars recognize new peremptory norms that forbid merely debatable (but not egregious) domestic conduct, the less those norms will retain their legitimacy as measures reserved for exceptional cases.

## Collaborate and Act

The United States and its partners should be less hesitant to employ international law when addressing genuinely transnational concerns and threats. Indeed, the formal instruments of international law must be updated to handle modern threats to state sovereignty. Over the long run, containing security threats will require drafting and updating reciprocal, consent-based legal instruments—such as treaties, conventions, and charters—to recognize modern threats to sovereignty that do not fall neatly into existing categories. Because of the stateless and transnational nature of terrorism, the United States must collaborate with its partners to construct an international regime that prevents nations from exporting their security risks.

Such a legal framework will apply most readily to activities that are inherently transnational and thus properly subject to the development of international standards. Take, for example, activities involving the transport of goods, people, or money from one country to another—such as air travel, cargo transportation, and cross-border financial transactions. International law is particularly appropriate for regulating such activities due to their quintessentially international character. No single country has either the capacity or the jurisdictional reach to control all global threats.

In many cases, the United States will be best able to address these fundamentally transnational security issues through bilateral agreements that synchronize U.S. security policies with those of other nations—as did the 2007 agreement between the European Union and the United States on sharing airline passenger name records (PNR). However, as more countries realize the security benefits of such bilateral arrangements, it may be appropriate to enlist all the United States' international partners in drafting multilateral frameworks that more widely synchronize states' security practices. These agreements would create minimum baselines of acceptable security measures aimed at activities originating in one country but directly affecting others. A group of nations could agree, for instance, to add provisions to the Convention on International Civil Aviation requiring that governments collect and share basic information about passengers. Similarly, they could draft a convention that establishes minimum screening procedures for cargo transported internationally. The fundamental goal of these new agreements would be to achieve containment through reciprocity. By agreeing to screen for outgoing threats originating within their own borders, individual countries would gain assurance that similar measures would be taken against incoming threats originating outside their borders.

Under this revised framework, both domestic and international institutions would play an important role in advancing security by enforcing new conventions on cargo security, transportation security, and other issues. International law would fill the legal gaps exploited by globally mobile terrorists and other such criminals.

To be sure, devising a truly collaborative and enforceable set of consent-based security obligations will take time. But there is reason for optimism. The international community has already begun tackling some classically transnational problems; recognition of the need for reciprocal security obligations is emerging in international criminal law. The UN Convention on the Law of the Sea adopted in 1988, for example, established a legal mechanism for delivering piracy offenders to signatory coastal nations and required that those nations prosecute or extradite such offenders. And in August 2006, the U.S. Senate approved the Convention on Cybercrime, which sets forth a comprehensive framework for international cooperation against computer crimes and requires member states to outlaw specific activities. These international agreements recognize that the unbounded nature of many illicit activities obliges individual states to cooperate to contain emerging threats and that the agreements themselves will only be successful if they are adopted with the consent of those states.

## Sovereignty Reciprocated

What should the international community do when global threats originate entirely within a state that does not consent to reciprocal international security obligations? This can occur when, for example, a nation fails to enact adequate domestic security measures or is simply unable to control terrorists or other criminals within a particular region. These situations present truly hard cases because they place the international community's security interests in conflict with a nation's right to control its internal matters. But states can no longer refuse to act by hiding behind seventeenth-century concepts of sovereignty in a world of twenty-first-century dangers. International law should not be powerless to prevent deadly nonstate threats from spreading from one state to others. If it is, the sovereignty of all nations will be sacrificed to preserve the sovereignty of one.

Therefore, international law must be updated to reflect the reciprocal nature of sovereignty in the modern era. As one example of the need for a new legal framework, consider the Charter of the United Nations, born from the experience of World War II. The Charter does not contemplate complex threats to sovereignty posed by transnational terrorist organizations, providing (in Article 2) only that "all Members shall refrain … from the threat or use of force against the territorial integrity or political independence of any state." And although Article 51 recognizes states' "inherent right of individual or collective self-defence" if attacked, some—as did the ICJ in the Israeli barrier case—narrowly interpret this self-defense exception to mean that a state can only exercise its right to self-defense if an imminent or actual attack on its territory comes from another nation-state, not a nonstate actor.

Such a narrow conception of self-defense misses the mark. As a practical matter, it ignores the increasing danger posed by nonstate actors, particularly in an age when they can obtain weapons of real destructive force. Moreover, it leaves nations helpless when an attack is threatened by a group that has created a haven within another state. Since the government of the host state is not itself launching an attack, Article 51 does not seem to come into play under the readings by ICJ and others. Yet from the standpoint of the targeted state, there is no meaningful difference between an attack launched by a government and an attack launched by terrorists whom a government has failed to control. NATO recognized this very fact when, after 9/11, it invoked the collective defense provision of its charter for the first time in its history. There remains, however, considerable ambiguity and disagreement concerning whether that provision and other international self-defense provisions apply to terrorists, and in what circumstances. The interior ministers of the six most populous EU member states in 2008 concluded that it is "important to explore the issue of self-defence fighting against terrorist targets in order to determine to what extent further tools, procedures and international legal cooperation is required."[5]

The reality of modern threats supports the need for an international legal framework that would require states to contain the negative global consequences of domestically originating security threats. The UN Security Council has only just begun the difficult work of constructing such a framework. In the immediate aftermath of 9/11, it passed Resolution 1373, which directed all member states to prevent and criminalize terrorism and to "refrain from providing any form of support, active or passive," to terrorists. As the resolution itself acknowledged, however, nations need to go further: to "cooperate ... through bilateral and multilateral arrangements and agreements, to prevent and suppress terrorist attacks and take action against perpetrators of such acts." The development of such a new legal framework is still in its infancy. Indeed, it was despite the passage of Resolution 1373 that the ICJ later embraced its narrow interpretation of the self-defense exception.

It is not enough for a group of nations, such as the Security Council, to pass resolutions that prohibit states from supporting terrorists. If states fail to contain transnational threats, there must be an international legal regime that subjects them to potential sanctions or even, if necessary, military intervention aimed at neutralizing those threats. Far from signaling a retreat to unilateralism, this approach would require cooperation in building a new legal framework. The mechanisms and limits of such an international legal regime will require time and effort to construct; the alternative, however, is an ad hoc regime that either encourages a go-it-alone approach or results in international paralysis. Embracing this new framework would not amount to abandoning consent-based international law; rather, it would enhance it. By recognizing that modern technology, transport, and trade often propel the destructive consequences of one state's action or inaction far beyond its own territory, the new framework would help states defend their sovereignty against new security threats.

This is not to deny that there is a tension between the argument that international law should require states to implement reasonable measures to contain international security threats originating within their borders and the argument that international law should defer to domestic policies aimed at bolstering international security. The critical distinction here, however, is between fundamentally domestic security concerns affecting a single nation and truly global threats that affect other states and their citizens. Whether a nation is taking sufficient measures to contain international security threats originating within its borders is an international matter, but as long as a state is successful in containing such treats, how it chooses to do so is a domestic issue.

In recognition of this distinction, the new reciprocal containment principle would afford governments maximum discretion to implement domestic security policies, provided that they are consistent with that nation's obligations to respect the sovereignty of other nations. Of course, this discretion need not be absolute, even in purely domestic affairs. One can imagine situations that would demand the flexibility to confront truly draconian measures implemented by non-democratic means—situations involving, for example, violations of long-established *jus cogens* norms. But international law will be more widely accepted when it strives to preserve the autonomy and mutual consent of nations in achieving international goals. Conversely, those who seek to forcibly impose abstract concepts of universal values on purely domestic decisions are placing the legitimacy of international law at risk.

## For the Moment, Caution

Such a set of reciprocal security obligations is unlikely to be crafted in the near future, and the task should not be rushed. In the meantime, the United States and its partners should employ more narrowly sculpted agreements and partnerships to address immediate security challenges. The United States and its allies would be wise in the short run to embrace a cautious approach, one that allows international rules to emerge gradually through the observation of the actual practices of states (and their consequences) and one that supplements these rules with voluntary, nonbinding agreements and principles. Legal scholar and U.S. Court of Appeals judge José Cabranes has noted, "It is precisely *because* the United States takes the law seriously, and takes seriously the international legal obligations that it assumes, that its leaders are cautious and careful in their approach to new and complicated arrangements" (emphasis original).

In the immediate future, the United States can best secure itself by building international law from the bottom up. One example of that strategy in action is the Proliferation Security Initiative, a voluntary arrangement spearheaded by the United States to promote the interdiction of banned nuclear, chemical, and biological weapons and weapons technology. The PSI, whose adherents consist of more than 90 countries, outlines cooperative measures that these countries work to implement and establishes a set of interdiction principles that they agree to support. The PSI and similar initiatives provide reason for hope that even in the absence of new, formal legal obligations, containment policies can indeed be based on consent. In fact, relying on informal commitments and actual state practice in the short term may offer an advantage: it will allow for a new, legitimate body of customary international law to emerge in an area in which little established custom or state practice currently exists.

The time has come to dispense with two prevailing, and contradictory, myths about international law: that it is necessarily antagonistic to U.S. interests, and that it is an inherently superior enterprise whose rules should trump policies adopted by democratically elected representatives. If the vitality of democratic principles is to be preserved, the United States must reject both of these extreme views and encourage its partners to help build a modern and sustainable international security framework—one based on the reciprocal responsibility to contain. Such a framework will fail if it overreaches by imposing binding rules prematurely or by subordinating cherished democratic principles to the prevailing normative winds. It will be more likely to succeed if it squarely addresses the new and dangerous threats to sovereignty that have emerged. In the end, only if the United States and its partners take a balanced and measured approach to these challenges will the legitimacy of the international legal system flourish.

# Conclusion: Before September 11—and Since

Since its creation in 2003, the Department of Homeland Security has achieved much in its efforts to enhance the safety and security of the United States. In the short span of its existence, the department has built a critical set of capabilities that were not in place prior to September 11.

- Before September 11, the United States had no effective system for identifying dangerous individuals arriving at our ports of entry. Today we can validate identities in seconds.

- Before September 11, the country did not have a coherent strategy for securing our land borders. Today, by applying a combination of increased manpower, pedestrian and vehicle fencing, and new technology, we do.

- Before September 11, America did not scan cargo entering its seaports for radiation. But today, we scan nearly 100 percent so we can prevent dangerous weapons from entering the country.

- Before September 11, the nation did not have national standards to protect chemical plants from attacks or to ensure that lethal chemicals did not fall into the wrong hands. Today, we have implemented tough new security standards that will protect chemical facilities as well as chemicals in transit.

- Before September 11, we did not have an effective aviation security regimen. Today, we have in place nearly two dozen layers of protection, from hardened cockpit doors to federal air marshals to 100 percent screening of passengers and their baggage.

- Finally, prior to 9/11, we did not have an effective emergency preparedness and response system. We have since rebuilt and reinvigorated the Federal Emergency Management Agency. And we have engaged the American people in an unprecedented nationwide effort to build a culture of preparedness.

These are some of the reasons our nation is now safer and better prepared to confront the challenges of the twenty-first century. Nonetheless, as I have outlined throughout this volume, serious challenges remain.

From border protection to disaster preparedness, from cyber security to biodefense, the Department of Homeland Security, in concert with its partners here and overseas, must continue its progress, confronting emergent threats, typically of a global nature, in a decisive, forward-looking fashion. As the nation faces these challenges, it will continue to rely on the 218,000 men and women of DHS. During my time as secretary, I never ceased to be inspired by my dedicated colleagues and partners who spent their days thinking about how they can better protect us all.

Today, their department remains anchored on a firm foundation.

While it has had its undeniable share of growing pains, it retains the proper combination of missions and capabilities that include not only countering threats like terrorism, but responding to and recovering from natural emergencies as well.

It is essential that future administrations work closely and diligently with these homeland security professionals. They must draw from their knowledge and experience, spur them to build on past successes, and provide them the necessary tools to keep delivering for this country and its people.

Congress can help by streamlining its homeland security oversight responsibilities. Currently, nearly 90 congressional committees and subcommittees oversee the department. With this many overseers, on a given day, there is a good chance that someone at DHS is being asked to testify before at least one of them. Clearly, it is the continued resolve of the people of DHS that helps keep their fellow Americans safe. Yet I am constantly reminded how it is the resolve of their fellow Americans on which they depend.

Looking ahead, the greatest threat we face is a faltering of this resolve, and the subtle encroachment of complacency. Make no mistake: in a post-9/11 world, complacency is a luxury that we can ill afford. How can future administrations combat it? They must continue to be candid with the American people, sharing as much information as possible about the dangers we face and the nature of our enemies.

What can ordinary Americans do? They can continue to take note of anything unusual in their environment and respond accordingly. Businesses can also do their part to make the country secure and safer. They can invest more in security and take stronger steps to protect their critical assets and infrastructure. Americans from all walks of life can become more educated consumers of information about national security. They can follow more closely the public dialogue. They can follow events, abroad as well as at home, more avidly. I believe strongly that the more informed they become, the more likely they will back sensible, risk-based security measures.

Last, while our principal goal is to prevent man-made disasters such as terrorist attacks from happening, individuals and their families can and should make preparedness plans just in case an incident—be it an attack or a natural disaster—occurs. I would continue to urge that every American do three things: assemble an emergency kit that includes food, water, first aid, and other essentials; make a family emergency plan; and learn about the different kinds of emergencies and how to respond to them.

As my successor, Janet Napolitano, pursues the challenging task of protecting the homeland, it is my hope that when her tenure has ended, she will pass on to her successor an even stronger, better department, one that has served our country well.

# Notes

## Introduction

1. See National Commission on Terrorist Attacks upon the United States, Thomas H. Kean, and Lee H. Hamilton, *The 9/11 Commission Report: Final Report of the National Commission on Terrorist Attacks Upon the United States* (New York: Norton, 2004) (cited throughout as *9/11 Report*).

## Chapter 1. Assessing the Dangers

1. J. Michael McConnell, Annual Threat Assessment of the Director of National Intelligence for the Senate  Select Committee on Intelligence, 5 February 2008.
2. Salman al Oudah, Ramadan Letter to Osama bin Laden, live broadcast, MBC Television, 14 September 2007.
3. See "Al-Qaeda's al-Zawahiri Repudiates Dr. Fadl's 'Rationalization of Jihad,'" *Terrorism Focus*, 30 April  2008.
4. Richard L. Armitage, "America's Challenges in a Changed World," remarks to U.S. Institute of Peace, Washington, D.C., 5 September 2002.

## Chapter 2. Ideological Roots

1. Director General of the Security Service Jonathan Evans, speech to Society of Editors, "A Matter of Trust" conference, Manchester, England, 5 November 2007.

2. Bernard Lewis, "License to Kill: Usama bin Ladin's Declaration of Jihad," *Foreign Affairs* 77 (November–December 1998): 19, cited by Ladan Boroumand and Roya Boroumand, "Terror, Islam, and Democracy," *Journal of Democracy* 13 (April 2002): 12.

3. "Message from the Lion Shaykh, Usama Bin Ladin, May God Protect him, to the American People," August–September 2007, video by Al-Sahab, media arm of Al Qaeda, selected video available at www.opensource.gov.

4. Osama bin Laden, May 1998 interview with John Miller of ABC News.

5. Ward Churchill, "Some People Push Back: On the Justice of Roosting Chickens," 12 September 2001, supplement to *Dark Night Field Notes, Pockets of Resistance* 11

6. Richard Stengel, "Osama bin Laden and the Idea of Progress," *Time*, 21 December 2001.

7. Clark Judge, "Urgency on the Battlefield," *Hoover Digest* 1 (2007).

8. Lawrence Wright, "The Rebellion Within," *New Yorker*, 2 June 2008.

9. Daniel Pipes, "The Western Mind of Radical Islam," *First Things* (December 1995).

10. There are, of course, variations of religious beliefs among Muslims, as in other religions, which promote differing views about the role of religion in daily life. Besides the well-known division between Sunni and Shi'a, there are streams within Islam that include what one academic has termed "the [largely Sufi] mystics" and "the modernists." See Akbar Ahmed, *Journey into Islam: The Crisis of Globalization* (Washington, D.C.: Brookings Institution Press, 2007).

11. Efraim Karsh, *Islamic Imperialism: A History* (New Haven, Conn.: Yale University Press), cited by Judge, "Urgency on the Battlefield."

12. Richard P. Mitchell, *The Society of the Muslim Brothers* (London:

Oxford University Press, 1969), 29, cited by Boroumand and Boroumand, "Terror, Islam, and Democracy," 7.

13. Matthias Kuntzel, "Jew-Hatred and Jihad: The Nazi Roots of the
9/11 Attack," *Weekly Standard* 13, 1 (17 September 2007).

14. For discussion see Walid Mahmoud Abdelnasser, *The Islamic Movement in Egypt: Perceptions of International Relations, 1967-81* (London: Kegan Paul, 1994), 173, cited in Pipes, "The Western Mind of
Radical Islam."

15. Mark Erikson, "Islamism, Fascism, and Terrorism (Part 2)," *Asian
Times Online*, 8 November 2002, http://www.atimes.com/atimes/
printN.html.

16. Boroumand and Boroumand, "Terror, Islam, and Democracy," 11.

17. Mark Erikson, "Islamism, Fascism, and Terrorism (Part 3)," *Asian
Times Online*, 4 December 2002, http://www.atimes.com/atimes/
printN.html.

18. Karam Zuhdi, a pioneer in recanting Islamist terrorism, claims that
as late as 2000, when he turned against violence, the Brotherhood
criticized it as "weakness." See Wright, "The Rebellion Within." As
Maajid Nawaz and others have noted, the big question continues to
be not only who has renounced terrorism, but how to treat those
who have done so but remain energetic advocates for the radical ideology and totalitarian aims of Islamism, as opposed to Islam.

19. Boroumand and Boroumand, "Terror, Islam, and Democracy," 9.

20. Ibid., 10.

21. The text of bin Laden's fatwa can be found at http://www.pbs.org/
newshour/terrorism/international/fatwa_1998.html

22. Winston Churchill, "The Sinews of Peace," address at Westminster
College, Fulton, Missouri, 5 March 1946.

23. Ronald Reagan, Remarks at the dedication of the Cold War Memorial, Westminster College, Fulton, Missouri, 9 November 1990.


## Chapter 3. Securing the Border

1. Comprehensive Immigration Reform Act, S.1348 (2007).

2. White House Office of the Press Secretary, "Fact Sheet: Improving

Border Security and Immigration Within Existing Law," http://www. whitehouse.gov/news/releases/2007.

3. "Southwest Border Fence," Department of Homeland Security, http://www.dhs.gov/xprevprot/programs/border-fence-southwest.shtm.

4. "U.S. Border Patrol," U.S. Customs and Border Protection, http://www.cbp.gov/xp/cgov/border_security/border_patrol/.

5. U.S. Customs and Border Protection News Room, "Securing America's Border—CBP 2008 Fiscal Year in Review," U.S. Customs and Border Protection, http://www.cbp.gov/xp/cgov/newsroom/highlights/08year_review.xml.

6. Jeffery Passel and D'Vera Cohn, "Trends in Unauthorized Immigration," Pew Hispanic Center, http://pewhispanic.org/reports/report.php?ReportID=94.

7. "Operation Community Shield: Targeting Violent Transnational Street Gangs," U.S. Immigrations and Customs Enforcement, http://www.ice.gov/pi/investigations/comshield/.

8. U.S. Immigration and Customs Enforcement Press Office, "ICE Fugitive Operations Program," http://www.ice.gov/pi/news/factsheets/nfop_fs.htm?searchstring=fugitive.

9. U.S. Immigration and Customs Enforcement Press Office, "297 Convicted and Sentenced Following ICE Worksite Operations in Iowa," http://www.ice.gov/pi/news/newsreleases/articles/080515waterloo.htm.

10. U.S. Immigration and Customs Enforcement Press Office, "Worksite Enforcement," http://www.ice.gov/pi/news/factsheets/worksite.htm.

11. "E-Verify," U.S. Citizenship and Immigration Services, http://www.uscis.gov/everify.

12. "Destination USA," Department of State, http://www.unitedstatesvisas.gov/.

13. "Portal," U.S. Citizenship and Immigration Services, http://www.uscis.gov/portal/site/uscis.

## Chapter 4. Using Every Tool

1. Press Release, "The White House, Setting the Record Straight: Iraq

Is the Central Front of Al Qaeda's Global Campaign," 3 May 2007, http://www.whitehouse.gov/news/releases/2007/.

2. See, e.g., Sudarsan Raghavan, "Sunni Factions Split with Al Qaeda Group: Rift Further Blurs Battle Lines in Iraq," *Washington Post*, 14 April 2007, A1.

3. See Ian Black, "Al-Qaida Deputy Goes Online to Justify Attacks, *Guardian*, 4 April 2008, 22.

4. See, e.g., U.S. Department of Homeland Security, Press Release, 9/11 Anniversary Progress and Priorities, 10 September 2008, http://www.dhs.gov/xnews/releases/pr_1221078411384.shtm.

5. See ibid.

6. See, e.g., U.S. Department of Homeland Security, National Infrastructure Protection Plan (2006), http://www.dhs.gov/xlibrary/assets/NIPP_Plan.pdf.

7. See, e.g., Dan Eggen, "Air Plot Said to Target Cities," *Washington Post*, 2 November 2006, A7.

8. Derek Chollet and James Goldgeier, *America Between the Wars: From 11/9 to 9/11* (New York: Public Affairs Books, 2008), xvi.

9. Charles Krauthammer, Op-Ed., "History Will Judge," *Washington Post*, 19 September 2008, A19.

10. Office of the Director of National Intelligence, "National Intelligence Estimate: The Terrorist Threat to the U.S. Homeland" (2007), http://dni.gov/press_releases/20070717_release.pdf.

11. Seth G. Jones and Martin C. Libicki, *How Terrorist Groups End: Lessons for Countering Al Qa'ida* (Santa Monica, Calif.: Rand, 2008), xvii.

12. Editorial, "The Moussaoui Mess," *Washington Post*, 29 September 2003, A18.

13. Editorial, "*U.S. v. Zacarias Moussaoui*," *Washington Post*, 12 December 2001, A34 ("The fact that the indictment was filed in U.S. District Court—not before a military commission— . . . is encouraging").

14. Editorial, "A Way Out," *Washington Post*, 4 October 2003, A18.

15. See Department of Justice Oversight: Preserving our Freedoms While Defending Against Terrorism: Hearings Before the Senate Committee on the Judiciary, 107th Cong. 10-15 (2001) (statement of

Michael Chertoff, Assistant Attorney General, Criminal Division, U.S. Department of Justice).

16. See, e.g., Convention for the Protection of Human Rights and Fundamental Freedoms, 4 November 1950, 213 U.N.T.S. 221; *Soering v. United Kingdom*, 11 Eur. Ct. H.R. 439 (1989) (prohibiting extradition of a German national from the United Kingdom to the United States for a capital murder trial, holding that such extradition would violate the prohibition against torture in Article 3 of the Convention in light of possible imposition of the death penalty).

17. Duncan Gardham, "Osama's Right-Hand Man, Abu Qatada, Back on the Streets," *Daily Telegraph*, 11 July 2008, 11 (describing release of a terrorism advocate illegally present in the UK).

18. *Othman v. Sec'y of State*, (2004) no. SC/15/2002 (UK Special Immigration Appeals Commission), http://www.siac.tribunals.gov.uk/Documents/outcomes/documents/sc152002qatada.pdf; see also Rosa Prince, "Still Here: 24 Terrorism Suspects Listed for Deportation," *Daily Telegraph*, 18 August 2008, 10 (noting Abu Qatada's continued presence in the UK).

19. See Richard Ford, "Bin Laden's 'Right-Hand Man' Wins Deportation Fight over Torture Fears," *Times* (London), 10 April 2008, 2.

## Chapter 5. Why Soft Power Works

1. See "Tsunami Relief Giving," Center on Philanthropy, Indiana University, January 2006, http://www.philanthropy.iupui.edu/Research/Giving/tsunami_relief_giving.aspx.

2. "Poll: Major Change of Public Opinion in Muslim World," Terror Free Tomorrow, February 2005, http://www.terrorfreetomorrow.org/articlenav.php?id=56.

3. *USAID Afghanistan*, 1 June 2003.

## Chapter 6. Why Washington Won't Work

1. See generally Amy B. Zegart, *Spying Blind: The CIA, the FBI, and the Origins of 9/11* (Princeton, N.J.: Princeton University Press, 2007), 85.
2. See generally Steven Emerson, *American Jihad: The Terrorists Living Among Us* (New York: Simon and Schuster, 2003), 148-49.
3. *9-11 Report*, 70, 190–91.
4. U.S. Commission on National Security in the 21st Century, Phase I Report, *New World Coming: American Security in the 21st Century* (Washington, D.C.: the Commission, 1999), 4, http://govinfo.library. unt.edu/nssg/Reports/NWC.pdf.
5. *9-11 Report*, 72. See also *United States v. Rahman*, 189 F.3d 88, 109, 123–27 (2d Cir. 1999) (detailing planning of the plot to bomb the Holland and Lincoln Tunnels and the UN, upholding jury verdict in relation to the conspiracy to bomb the landmarks).
6. David Johnston, "Few Answers About Man Being Held in Bomb Case," *New York Times*, 21 December 1999, A24.
7. See generally DHS, US-VISIT, http://www.dhs.gov/xabout/structure/gc_1190896326320.shtm.
8. Shane Harris, "Bush Orders FBI, CIA to Build New Terror Intelligence Office," *GovernmentExecutive*, 29 January 2003, http://www.govexec.com/dailyfed/0103/012903h1.htm (accessed 8 December 2008).
9. Eric Chabrow, "U.S. Will Fingerprint Foreign Visitors Who Need Visas," *InformationWeek*, 19 May 2003, http://www.informationweek.com/news/software/showArticle.jhtml?articleID=1000027.
10. *9-11 Report*, 401.
11. See Howard Kunreuther and Doug Easterling, "The Role of Compensation in Siting Harzardous Facilities," *Journal of Policy Analysis and Management* 15 (Autumn 1996): 601.
12. Patrick O'Driscoll, Steve Wieberg, Peter Eisler, and Rick Hampson, "Inside City, the Deluge Came After the Storm," *USA Today*, 6 September 2005, 10A.
13. John Schwartz, "Big, Maybe Ugly, But Their Role Heroic," *New York Times*, 23 March 2006, A18.

## Chapter 10. Managing Identity

1. Miriam Jordan, "How to Make Identity Theft Worse," *Wall Street Journal*, 7 Auguast 2008.

## Chapter 12. Biological Effects

1. Commission on the Prevention of Weapons of Mass Destruction Proliferation and Terrorism, *World at Risk* (New York: Vintage, 2008).
2. See statement by Al Qaeda spokesman Suleiman Abu Gheith, quoted in MEMRI Special Dispatch 388, 12 June 2002.

## Chapter 13. The Question of FEMA and Homeland Security

1. Joseph Lieberman and Susan Collins, "LETTER; Reforming FEMA: Two Senators Speak Out," *New York Times*, 10 December 2008.
2. "Management of Domestic Incidents," Homeland Presidential Security Directive HSPD-5, 28 February 2003.

## Chapter 14. Cooperation and Consensus Abroad

1. London Metropolitan Police Deputy Assistant Commissioner Peter Clarke, "Learning from Experience—Counter Terrorism in the UK Since 9/11," first Colin Cramphorn Memorial Lecture, Policy Exchange, London, 24 April 2007.
2. *Economist*, 24 November 2007.

## Chapter 15. The Responsibility to Contain

1. Philippe Sands, *Lawless World: America and the making and breaking of Global Rules from FDR's Atlantic Charter to George Bush's Illegal War* (New York: Viking, 2005), Preface.

2. Louis B. Sohn, "Sources of International Law," *Georgia Journal of International and Comparative Law* 25 (1995–96): 401.
3. Robert Kagan, "The September 12 Paradigm: America, the World, and George W. Bush," *Foreign Affairs* (September–October 2008).
4. For example, Commission on Human Rights Resolution 2003/4.
5. Meeting of the Interior Ministers of Germany, France, Italy, Poland, Spain, the United Kingdom and the Secretary of Homeland Security of the United States of America, 26–27 September 2008, Villa Hammerschmidt, Bonn.

# Index

# Acknowledgments

I WOULD like to dedicate this book to the brave men and women at the U.S. Department of Homeland Security, whom I was honored and privileged to lead during my time as Secretary. Our country owes them a great debt of gratitude for their outstanding service and unwavering commitment to making us safer while maintaining our freedom. This book is also dedicated to all the DHS families, including my own wonderful wife and children, for their loyal support, patience, and understanding in light of the significant time challenges involved in protecting the homeland.

I would also like to thank some key individuals for making this volume a reality.

I want to commend Paul Rosenzweig for conceiving the notion of making our mission and strategy the subject of a book to help educate the country on the nature of our continued challenges and how we must meet them today and in the future.

I want to thank Paul Liben for his contributions at each stage in the process and particularly for his "wordsmithing," strategizing, and help in seeing this project through to completion.

And of course I want to thank Bill Finan and his stellar team at the University of Pennsylvania Press for their indispensable role in turning our manuscript into this volume.

This book is an edited and revised collection of key speeches delivered and articles written in commemoration of the fifth anniversary of DHS.

Chapter 1 is adapted from "Confronting Threats to the Homeland: The Next Generation," *Yale Journal of International Affairs* (Spring/Summer 2008).

Chapter 2 is adapted from "The Ideology of Terror: Radicalism Revisited," *Brown Journal of World Affairs* (November–December 2008) and "The Battle for Our Common Future," *Journal of International Security Affairs* (Spring 2008).

Chapter 3 is adapted from "Homeland Security and Immigration: An Impetus for Reform," *LBJ Journal of Public Affairs* (2009).

Chapter 4 is adapted from "Tools Against Terror: All of the Above," *Harvard Journal of Law & Public Policy* 32, no. 1 (Winter 2009).

Chapter 5 is adapted from "Preventing Terrorism: A Case for Soft Power," *Harvard International Review* (Summer 2008).

Chapter 6 is adapted from "Why Washington Won't Work: Structural Obstacles in Post-9/11 America," *Georgetown Journal of Law and Public Policy* (2009).

ACKNOWLEDGMENTS

Chapter 7 is adapted from "Preserving Infrastructure: A 21st Century Challenge," *Parameters* (Winter 2008–9).

Chapter 8 is adapted from "The Cybersecurity Challenge," *Regulation and Governance* (December 2008).

Chapter 10 is adapted from "Managing Identity: A Global Challenge," *Orbis* (Winter 2009).

Chapter 11 is adapted from "A Strategic Approach to Risk Management," *Fletcher Forum* (2009).

Chapter 12 is adapted from "Confronting Biological Threats to the Homeland," *Joint Forces Quarterly* (4th Quarter 2008).

Chapter 14 is adapted from "Transatlantic Convergence on Passenger Data Questions," *European Affairs* (Winter/Spring 2008).

Chapter 15 is adapted from "The Responsibility to Contain: Protecting Sovereignty under International Law," *Foreign Affairs* (January/February 2009).